D0063752

I Still
BELIEVE

The most difficult aspect of life is enduring trials of any kind. From cover to cover, one of the strongest themes threaded throughout Scripture is holding onto God when suffering comes into our lives. The *I Still Believe* Journal is a five-week journey into discovering his strength in our darkest moments.

Table of

"WHEREVER THIS GOES, I'M ALL IN"

In this world you
will have trouble.
But take heart! I have
overcome the world.

-JOHN 16:33

S tress. Pressure. Crazy schedules. The chaotic normal.

Disappointments. Letdowns. Hurts. The ever-struggling state of our fragile hearts.

Every single day, we deal with first-world problems like the car not starting at the worst possible time or spilling a five-dollar cup of coffee in the car. But we also face the real crises that bring life to a sudden halt through a doctor's diagnosis that no one saw coming or a midnight phone call with devastating news.

In the news and on social media, we see the world around us in a state of hopelessness. The abuse of painkillers is classified as an epidemic. Suicide rates are rising among the young at the time they should be thriving into their future. Anxiety from within and anger towards the external are rampant. Our culture is desperately seeking answers while battling the fact that the questions keep changing.

As Christ-followers, when we begin to look intently into the Word of God for answers, we often find what can be perceived as oxymorons, like "living sacrifice." We discover strange metaphors like "faith as small as a mustard seed that can move mountains," along with cultural contradictions such as "whoever loses their life will find it."

While the world's paradigms have always struggled with a response to a God of love versus the bad things that happen to humans, Jesus appeared and made head-scratching statements like:

"IN THIS WORLD YOU
WILL HAVE TROUBLE. BUT
TAKE HEART! I HAVE
OVERCOME THE WORLD."

- JOHN 16:33

"BLESSED ARE YOU
WHEN PEOPLE INSULT
YOU, PERSECUTE YOU
AND FALSELY SAY ALL
KINDS OF EVIL AGAINST
YOU BECAUSE OF
ME. REJOICE AND BE
GLAD ...

-MATTHEW 5:11-12

Yet over and over again, Jesus reminded us: "Don't be afraid." In Mark 5:36 and Luke 8:50, he added another encouragement: "Don't be afraid; just believe."

So according to Jesus, belief is a counteraction to fear. But how does belief change us? Can simple belief actually change us?

One answer to these questions is found in the first chapter of the Book of James. But the disclaimer in these verses can be a struggle to wrap our twenty-first-century brains around.

CONSIDER IT PURE JOY,
MY BROTHERS AND
SISTERS, WHENEVER
YOU FACE TRIALS OF
MANY KINDS, BECAUSE
YOU KNOW THAT THE
TESTING OF YOUR
FAITH PRODUCES
PERSEVERANCE. LET
PERSEVERANCE FINISH
ITS WORK SO THAT YOU
MAY BE MATURE AND
COMPLETE, NOT
LACKING ANYTHING. ...
BLESSED IS THE ONE
WHO PERSEVERES
UNDER TRIAL BECAUSE,

> HAVING STOOD THE TEST, THAT PERSON WILL RECEIVE THE CROWN OF LIFE THAT THE LORD HAS PROMISED TO THOSE WHO LOVE HIM.
>
> - JAMES 1:2-4, 12

So in response to this fallen world and all the crises created in this life, if we are going to not only believe God's Word, but also apply his truth to transform us, then we must also accept the supernatural progression James offers us:

- Pure joy is available as we face any trial.
- Trials test our faith and can create a godly perseverance.
- Such perseverance will produce maturity and completeness.
- This refining-under-fire brings life that only God can produce in us—not lacking anything.

Jeremy Camp's testimony and story of life, love, and faith about he and his wife's battle with cancer are beautifully and poignantly shared in the film *I Still Believe*. While the deeply personal turmoil was constant, Jeremy displayed an unwavering faith in Christ, believing for Melissa's healing, while navigating his own calling to minister to others through Christian music. Their fight together to overcome overwhelming odds ultimately created a profound struggle and placed Jeremy at a crossroads of walking forward in trusting God or turning his back on his faith.

This is the same choice we will all face someday in our own circumstances, if we haven't already.

The story of *I Still Believe* overlays over the blueprint of the James 1 passage to see the meeting of Heaven and Earth for God to be glorified, and ultimately for Jeremy to be sent out to tell their story, reaching millions of people with the Gospel.

Had Jeremy chosen to not persevere in Christ, there would be no story to tell today.

So the great truth from the film that we desire to share with you in these pages is simply this: When you choose to persevere in your relationship with Jesus, God will create a story from your life to reach people no one else could. That is the calling of every Christ-follower.

May you echo to Jesus what Jeremy told Melissa in the hospital following her cancer diagnosis: "Wherever this goes, I'm all in."

Blessed is the one who perseveres.

Blessed is the one who confesses, "*I still believe.*"

HOW TO USE THIS JOURNAL

The concepts of faith and belief battling our everyday fears and doubts are always challenging to navigate. Finding joy in our trials and peace in our storms can be a tough road to walk, even for veteran Christ-followers. That is exactly why we have produced the *I Still Believe* Journal. We want this 35-day journey to help you accelerate your spiritual maturity and bring a fresh wave of growth to your faith in Christ.

This Study Journal involves a commitment of five weeks. Each week has five days of content and interaction, a sixth day as a "Call to Action", and a seventh day for catch-up, review, along with preparation and prayer for your small group, if applicable to your situation.

For days one through five, you'll read a devotional based on Scripture and the themes of *I Still Believe*. Connecting stories and quotes from Jeremy and Adrienne Camp are also included. Some days will have specific messages from the film *I Still Believe* or a practical exercise to help you connect the content to what is happening in your own life. Following your reading of the day, you will work through the "Getting Personal" section. These questions are designed to help you go deeper with the study content.

For each of the 35 days, the goal is life transformation through God's power in your relationship with Christ. We also pray these five weeks will help you develop a daily pattern of Bible interaction and prayer.

If you are using this Journal in conjunction with the *I Still Believe* video episodes, watching each week's video BEFORE completing the Journal is recommended. For example, watch Episode 1, then complete Week 1 in the Journal.

While watching the *I Still Believe* movie is not necessary for completing this journal, seeing Jeremy and Melissa's story come to life on the screen will help you better connect with and understand the study. We suggest watching the film before you start the study if you choose to do so.

CALL TO ACTION

At the end of each week, you will be given a Call to Action. The goal of this section is to transition and transfer understanding into application. Several places throughout Scripture, God said he desires obedience over sacrifice. That's why the end goal of the Call to Action is practice and obedience.

Before starting Day One, complete these to help you get started:

WHERE YOU ARE

On a scale of one to ten—one being you are going through a serious faith struggle to ten being you are closer to God than ever before—how would you rate your spiritual walk today? Circle the number. The goal is simply to be honest about where you are, just between you and God.

1———2———3———4———5———6———7———8———9———10

Next, list some reasons why you rated yourself at that number on the scale.

_____

_____

_____

WHERE YOU WANT TO BE

Considering where you just rated yourself on the scale regarding your spiritual walk, what number would best represent where you would realistically like to be in five weeks following this study? Set a spiritual goal.

1———2———3———4———5———6———7———8———9———10

What do you believe it will take for you to get there?

_____

_____

_____

Lastly, if you are using this Journal as a part of a small group study, we want to encourage you to commit to and get to know the people in your group, if you don't know them already. Make the intentional decision to work hard, be disciplined, be proactive to pray for the people, and be accountable to them as well.

If you are using this Journal outside of a small group, consider forming your own with some friends and going through it together. If that is not possible, then ask a Christian friend to pray for you and offer accountability to you for the next five weeks.

1

YOU ARE
MY HOPE

Sacrifice

Day 1

A HOLY EXCHANGE

In *I Still Believe*, we see a clear and consistent pattern of Jeremy's parents and siblings, Melissa, Jean-Luc, and of course, Jeremy, all exhibiting sacrifice as not just occasional events but as part of their actual lifestyles. When we truly follow the One who became the ultimate sacrifice for the entire human race, our very lives will be marked by personal sacrifice for God and others.

The theme passage for this week is Hebrews 12:1-3. While the word "sacrifice" is not actually used in the verses, the entire truth presented here is that of giving up what you have for the sake of others to receive what only God can give. This is a holy exchange. Let's take this important passage apart sentence by sentence to best understand the meaning and connection for us.

A major factor in understanding this passage is that it immediately follows Hebrews 11, which has long been called the "Hall of Faith." The first word "therefore" connects to the idea that all of the folks in the Bible (v. 1-38), including all believers throughout the centuries (v. 39-40), create an amazing lineage as a historical, generational, and global heavenly community. We are never solo actors but rather constant participants with a unique place as a branch in an eternal family tree.

> THEREFORE, SINCE WE ARE SURROUNDED BY SUCH A GREAT CLOUD OF WITNESSES.
>
> - HEBREWS 12:1

LET US THROW OFF EVERYTHING THAT HINDERS
AND THE SIN THAT SO EASILY ENTANGLES. AND LET
US RUN WITH PERSEVERANCE THE RACE MARKED
OUT FOR US, FIXING OUR EYES ON JESUS, THE
PIONEER AND PERFECTER OF FAITH.

- HEBREWS 12:1-2

The writer of Hebrews was encouraging a persecuted group of Christ-followers, a reality most of us in the Western church today cannot comprehend. He likened the faith journey to a race where the runners need to get rid of excess baggage to run in freedom; namely because the Christian life is a marathon, not a sprint or dash.

The writer then drew a parallel between the believers' persecution to Jesus's endurance of the cross. Because Christ finished his race and completed his work, he is at the end of our race as the goal upon which we focus. He is the reason we can get to the finish line at all and experience victory.

FOR THE JOY SET BEFORE HIM HE ENDURED THE
CROSS, SCORNING ITS SHAME, AND SAT DOWN AT
THE RIGHT HAND OF THE THRONE OF GOD.

- HEBREWS 12:2

The greatest trial of all time was Christ's sacrifice on the cross. Yet during his trial, beating, and crucifixion, Jesus used his future joy as the motivation to endure the pain of the cross and the scorn of men. That joy culminated when he finally sat down forever in victory at the right hand of the Father. When we sacrifice and endure suffering, we take part in what Jesus did for us.

CONSIDER HIM WHO ENDURED SUCH OPPOSITION FROM SINNERS, SO THAT YOU WILL NOT GROW WEARY AND LOSE HEART.

- HEBREWS 12:3

Finally, we are given the example of Christ to overcome the obstacles that sin creates in our own journey to motivate and inspire us to stay courageous and stand strong here while we wait on Heaven.

> **"I love Hebrews 12:1-3 so much. 'For the joy set before him, he endured the cross.' In the sacrifice that Jesus made, we are the joy, as if he said, 'My love for them is so great that I'm willing to sacrifice my life because of the relationship that I can have with my children. If there's any other way, that'd be awesome, but not my will but your will be done for the greater purpose.'"**

JEREMY CAMP

THE SUFFERING SERVANT

At 52 years old, George Frideric Handel suffered a stroke that left his right arm paralyzed and his vision blurred. And because he had a habit of falling in and out of favor with British royalty in his day, his income was continually jeopardized. He eventually lost most of his money in the production of operas. By 1740, he was debilitated, depressed, and in debt.

One day Handel happened onto a libretto by Charles Jennens, composed entirely of Scripture. The three parts consisted of prophecies from Isaiah about the coming Messiah, the birth, life, ministry, death, and resurrection of Christ, and his final victory over sin and death from the book of Revelation. As Handel read the words, he was deeply moved.

Jennens' work inspired Handel to compose an oratorio. In the summer of 1741, he committed himself fully to putting Scripture to music. One day, his assistant found him in tears with Handel expressing, "I did think I saw heaven open, and saw the very face of God." The section he was writing at that moment was what became known as "The Hallelujah Chorus."

His finished work first premiered during the Easter season in April 1742 and changed Handel's life and legacy forever.

Handel took a great risk in the composition of the *Messiah* since no one was funding his work at the time. The months he spent putting music to Scripture could easily have been dedicated to writing another opera—what many would have viewed as a safer option. But his obvious drawing to the Gospel and his destitute disposition brought about an openness to sacrifice his time and reputation. The final result of his commitment was a strong personal connection to God and the birth of one of the most prolific masterpieces in music history. His work still honors Christ in sacred and secular venues all over the world today. ■

getting personal

HOW DOES GRASPING THE CONCEPT THAT WE ARE PART OF A BIGGER PICTURE, A LONG LEGACY OF FAITH, ENCOURAGE YOU IN YOUR OWN FAITH JOURNEY AND INSPIRE YOU TO MAKE YOUR OWN PERSONAL SACRIFICES?

WHAT DOES THE IMAGE OF A RUNNER WITH NO HINDRANCES, A CLEAR MOTIVATION, AND A GOAL SAY TO YOU ABOUT GOD'S HOPE FOR YOUR PERSONAL PERSEVERANCE?

WHAT IS ONE INSPIRATIONAL POINT YOU GLEANED FROM THE STORY OF HANDEL'S MESSIAH?

WHERE ARE YOU REGULARLY TEMPTED TO "FIX YOUR EYES" THAT DISTRACTS YOU FROM JESUS AND YOUR SPIRITUAL GOALS?

WHAT PHRASE IN HEBREWS 12:1-3 MOST STANDS OUT TO YOU? EXPLAIN.

REFLECT

HAS TODAY'S PRESENTATION ON SACRIFICE CHANGED YOUR SPIRITUAL PERSPECTIVE IN ANY WAY? EXPLAIN.

IN CLOSING TODAY, USE HEBREWS 12:1-3 AS A PERSONAL CONFESSION AND PRAYER, WRITING IN THE BLANKS WHAT GOD LEADS YOU TO SACRIFICE TO HIM TODAY. THEN PRAY THE WORDS AS YOUR OWN.

[LORD JESUS], SINCE [I AM] SURROUNDED BY SUCH A GREAT CLOUD OF WITNESSES, LET [ME] THROW OFF_____ AND _____ THAT SO EASILY ENTANGLES [ME]. [HELP ME] RUN WITH PERSEVERANCE THE RACE MARKED OUT FOR [ME], FIXING [MY] EYES ON [YOU], THE PIONEER AND PERFECTER OF [MY] FAITH. FOR THE JOY SET BEFORE [YOU], [YOU] ENDURED THE CROSS, SCORNING ITS SHAME, AND SAT DOWN AT THE RIGHT HAND OF THE THRONE OF GOD. [HELP ME TO REMEMBER YOU] ENDURED SUCH OPPOSITION FROM SINNERS, SO THAT [I] WILL NOT GROW WEARY AND LOSE HEART. IN YOUR NAME, AMEN.

CONSIDER REGULARLY USING THIS EXERCISE ANYTIME YOU NEED TO BE REMINDED OF YOUR TRUE GOAL IN YOUR FAITH JOURNEY.

Day 2

ACTING LIKE ABRAHAM

I n *I Still Believe*, Jeremy Camp had a choice to make when he learned of Melissa's diagnosis: ignore or engage, walk away or run into. His decision at that crossroad forever changed him and his relationship with Christ would never be the same. That is the nature of sacrifice in the kingdom of God.

ACTING LIKE ABRAHAM

In Genesis 22, God asked Abraham to take his beloved, promised son up to a mountain and sacrifice him. We read God's command in verse 2, and then in verses 3-10, amazingly, we are told of Abraham's exact obedience to the point of raising the knife to sacrifice his son. Verses 11-12 bring Isaac's deliverance.

BUT THE ANGEL OF THE LORD CALLED OUT TO HIM FROM HEAVEN, "ABRAHAM! ABRAHAM!" "HERE I AM," HE REPLIED. "DO NOT LAY A HAND ON THE BOY," HE SAID. "DO NOT DO ANYTHING TO HIM. NOW I KNOW THAT YOU FEAR GOD, BECAUSE YOU HAVE NOT WITHHELD FROM ME YOUR SON, YOUR ONLY SON."

JESUS KNEW HE WOULD BECOME
THE ULTIMATE SACRIFICE AND SO
HE HAD AUTHORITY FROM THE FATHER
TO OFFER A REPLACEMENT LAMB.

Two very important points in this passage are:

1. Verse 2 clearly states the command to sacrifice Isaac came from God. But in verse 11, the command to stop comes from "the angel of the Lord." Many theologians believe this reference, like others in the Old Testament that use similar language, is Christ. Jesus knew he would become the ultimate sacrifice and so he had the authority from the Father to offer a replacement of a ram for the offering, just as he would be the replacement for the sins of all humankind.

2. While Abraham did not ultimately have to sacrifice his only son, it would not be at all accurate to say he sacrificed nothing. He did indeed sacrifice his own desires, legacy, and will. He had to "put the knife to" those things before he could even take Isaac up the mountain. To Abraham, he put his entire life on that altar, and God honored his obedience.

Because of Jesus, we will never be asked to sacrifice our own "Isaac" as Abraham was. But every single day, God does ask us to sacrifice, just like Abraham in obedience. For God to be God in our lives, we must "put to death" our own desires and follow him, not going our own way.

REPLICA VS. REAL

A young lady who was about to graduate from high school had a very close relationship with her dad. He had ordered a diamond necklace to give her as a special keepsake to celebrate her achievement. The day before the big event, the dad received word that the necklace would be delayed several days. Having to improvise, he went to the jewelry counter at a retail store and bought an inexpensive cubic zirconia necklace that closely resembled the one he ordered. He decided when the real one arrived he would just explain what happened and exchange it with his daughter.

The morning of graduation as she was preparing to get ready, the dad asked his daughter what jewelry she was planning on wearing. Not suspecting anything, she excitedly told him about the earrings, bracelets, and rings she had laid out the night before. When she finished, the father asked, "You didn't mention a necklace?" She answered, "Dad, I don't really have a nice one for an occasion like this."

Her dad smiled and said, "Well, let's see about that," as he handed her the gift box. When she opened it and saw the necklace, she cried and kept hugging her dad, thanking him over and over.

For the next several days, she and her necklace were inseparable. Her response made the dad even more excited about giving her the real diamond necklace.

Finally, the package arrived. That night he walked into her room and explained the delay of her gift and what he had decided to do. He asked for the zirconia necklace back and offered her the real diamond one in exchange.

Surprised, she began to cry. Puzzled, the dad asked, "Honey, what's wrong? I gave you a necklace for graduation, but this is the real thing that I always wanted you to have." Grasping onto the necklace around her neck, she explained, "But, Dad, this is the one you gave me on that day. This one is special to me. Please don't ask me to give it up. I don't care what is real and what is a replica. Send the other one back. I don't want it."

While we can all be puzzled by the girl's reaction to keep the replica and not accept the real necklace, we do this ourselves when we hold onto the things of this world in place of what God wants to give us. We must sacrifice what we have for what he wants for our lives, exchange the old for the new, the replica for the real.

For example, a young man has been casually seeing a girl but then meets someone else he senses God strongly leading him toward. A woman has a job that pays very well, but then her true passion and calling that she always felt God would one day call her toward comes along, but the job pays less. A couple has been saving for a new car but then finds out about a family in dire need and feels compelled to give. A man has been looking forward to his day off to rest, but then a new friend he has been ministering to calls and asks for help to move. As Christ-followers, we face these decisions every day.

In a culture where affluence and comfort are highly valued, the concept of "sacrifice" can easily be ignored. While no one immediately signs up to sacrifice something, in the Christian experience, there are plenty of moments where the absolute best thing for us to do is give in and give up whatever God is asking.

"I feel the sacrifice kick in when I'm being stretched to my max, Jeremy is on the road, and I'm just exhausted with being a mom. I just get on my knees and pray, 'Okay, Lord, you've given us this life.' We've had to sacrifice a lot as a family. But because I know we're doing this for the greater good and Jeremy is not just out there entertaining is the key. I know he's out there ministering to people and sharing the good news of what God has done, sharing hope. He's sharing his testimony and people's lives are being impacted. When I'm at home stretched to my max exhausted, that's what makes it worth it."

ADRIENNE CAMP

EXERCISE

Put a check mark next to the things that you need to sacrifice or give over to God. Be as honest as possible.

- ☐ TIME
- ☐ SOCIAL MEDIA
- ☐ YOUR JOB
- ☐ TV
- ☐ ENTERTAINMENT
- ☐ MONEY
- ☐ WORRY
- ☐ FEAR
- ☐ ANXIETY
- ☐ DEPRESSION
- ☐ A RELATIONSHIP
- ☐ HEALTH

- ☐ YOUR IDENTITY
- ☐ YOUR TRUST
- ☐ YOUR HOPES
- ☐ ANGER
- ☐ BITTERNESS
- ☐ ILLNESS
- ☐ CONTROL
- ☐ YOUR HEART
- ☐ YOUR MIND
- ☐ DREAMS
- ☐ MATERIAL ITEMS
- ☐ WHAT OTHERS THINK

IN THE LEFT COUMN, WHAT THINGS ARE AFFECTING
YOUR RELATIONSHIP WITH GOD? WHAT DO YOU NEED
TO GIVE OR SACRIFICE TO GOD?

IN THE RIGHT COUMN, WHAT THINGS ARE AFFECTING
YOUR RELATIONSHIP WITH GOD? WHAT ARE SOME
PRACTICAL WAYS OF ADDRESSING THESE?

getting personal

WHAT PERSONAL BATTLES DO YOU SUPPOSE ABRAHAM FOUGHT BETWEEN GOD'S COMMAND AND RAISING THE KNIFE?

WHAT ARE YOUR THOUGHTS REGARDING THE IDEA THAT THE COMMAND CAME FROM GOD TO SACRIFICE ISAAC, BUT THE COMMAND TO STOP CAME FROM JESUS?

IN THE STORY ABOUT THE DAD'S GIFT FOR HIS DAUGHTER, HOW DID HER EMOTIONS IMPACT HER DECISION TO EXCHANGE THE REAL FOR THE REPLICA?

WHAT IS ONE SITUATION WHERE YOU KNOW GOD CALLED YOU TO
SACRIFICE WHAT YOU HAD IN EXCHANGE FOR WHAT HE HAS PLANNED
FOR YOU?

IS THERE A CHALLENGE YOU ARE FACING RIGHT NOW WHERE YOU
SENSE GOD IS CALLING YOU TO SOMETHING YOU FEEL MAY BE TOO
DIFFICULT FOR YOU? TAKE A MOMENT TO LIST OUT THE PROS AND
CONS OF THE SACRIFICE AND THEN WRITE DOWN WHAT YOU BELIEVE
GOD IS TRYING TO ACCOMPLISH IN YOU.

Day 3

THRONE VS. ALTAR

In Romans 12:1, we come across an oxymoron when Paul refers to being a "living sacrifice". The reason for this apparent mismatch is the very nature of a sacrifice refers to some living thing being put to death. A sacrifice is killed as a substitution for another. The sacrifice dies in place of someone who lives.

So once a "sacrifice" is made, how then can it continue to be "living"? Let's take a look at Paul's verse.

> THEREFORE, I URGE YOU, BROTHERS AND SISTERS, IN VIEW OF GOD'S MERCY, TO OFFER YOUR BODIES AS A LIVING SACRIFICE, HOLY AND PLEASING TO GOD—THIS IS YOUR TRUE AND PROPER WORSHIP.
>
> — ROMANS 12:1

God has made the ultimate display of his kindness, mercy, and grace to all, without exception, because of the sacrifice of his Son. Because of what Christ has done, there is no longer a need for any animal sacrifice or for another person to die in our place to take care of our sin before a holy God. Once we receive his great gift, our response should be to follow our Lord's example and voluntarily offer all of our lives.

Therefore, a living sacrifice has to actually remain on the altar 24 hours a day, all 365 days a year in an ever-present state of offering while continuing to live and

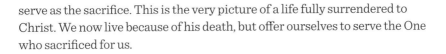

serve as the sacrifice. This is the very picture of a life fully surrendered to Christ. We now live because of his death, but offer ourselves to serve the One who sacrificed for us.

To offer an analogy for this biblical truth, in all our lives there is a throne and an altar. Christ left his throne to offer himself on the altar on our behalf. His act of obedience to the Father allows and empowers us to make the same choice.

When we surrender to God through a relationship with Jesus Christ, we choose to abdicate the throne of our lives to Jesus. In "view of God's mercy," we take our place on the altar as an act of "true and proper worship." Before Christ, we lived on *our* throne. Now in Christ, we live on *his* altar.

NATURAL VS. SUPERNATURAL

Still sinners, however, when we make the decision to get up off the altar to once again take the throne and rule our own lives, God brings conviction first and then circumstances to draw us back.

Our daily goal as believers is to stay off the throne of our lives where God belongs and live on the altar where we belong. This truth redefines worship as a lifestyle, living in holiness, and pleasing God in all we do. Our moments of public and private worship are to be opportunities for the ongoing expression of our hearts, not occasional events disconnected from the rest of our lives.

As sinners, life off the throne and on the altar is not natural—but supernatural—impossible apart from Christ. That's why for so many people, giving over control of their lives feels like an unwanted and impossible act.

When driving experts teach us about navigating our vehicles when we lose control on ice, the instruction they give is not at all natural. To avoid a wreck and survive, they tell us when the car begins to slide to *lightly* pump the brakes and steer *into* the direction of the skid. But what is our natural, initial, often panicked response when we are suddenly sliding off the road? Hurriedly turn the steering wheel back to the other direction and *slam* on the brakes! To stay safe, to not hurt anyone or incur damage, we must do the *opposite* of what *feels* like the natural reaction. The only way this will occur is for our training to kick in and take the appropriate response and action—the opposite of what *feels* right.

For us to be living sacrifices, we must continually give up our natural inclination to take back the throne. A life lived on his altar will never be easy but will always be the right choice for our *best* life.

> **"After seeing the movie *I Still Believe*, people will ask, 'Was you going off to college and the sacrifices made by your family real, like with giving you the guitar?' Yeah, that was real. Mom and Dad believed in what I was doing and what God was doing. There was a lot of sacrifice because they didn't really have the money. That was about their faith. Sacrifice was instilled in our family, stepping outside of our own preferences, learning to walk in that. When I went out to California and met Melissa—that innocent scene of me saying, 'Whatever this is, I'm willing to walk through it,' was out of the overflow of my heart. My love was real. Literally just a byproduct of understanding the sacrifice of what Christ did for us, how it changed our lives and us. It was just second nature."**

JEREMY CAMP

Using Jeremy's last line, a great response for us as Christians would be to deem our new "second nature" as the decision to live exactly as he indicated: committed to the sacrificial life. ■

are you committed
to the sacrificial life?

getting personal

WHAT DYNAMICS IN OUR LIFE AND CULTURE MAKE THE PHRASE "LIVING SACRIFICE" SEEM LIKE AN OXYMORON?

WHY SHOULD GOD'S GIFT AND CHRIST'S SACRIFICE FOR US MANDATE A RESPONSE FROM US?

WHAT ARE YOUR THOUGHTS ABOUT THE "THRONE AND ALTAR" CONCEPT?

WHY WOULD GOD CONTINUE TO OFFER THE ALTAR AS A CHOICE AFTER SALVATION WHEN HE COULD EASILY DEMAND OR EVEN FORCE OUR OBEDIENCE?

COMPLETE THESE OPEN-ENDED SENTENCES TO PROCESS YOUR LIFE ON THE ALTAR RIGHT NOW:

FATHER, MY GREATEST AREA OF STRUGGLE TO SACRIFICE IN OBEDIENCE TO YOU IS:

FATHER, A RECENT PLACE OF SURRENDER TO YOU THAT IS BECOMING "SECOND NATURE" IS:

Day 4

CONFORM OR TRANSFORM

Yesterday we focused on one very powerful verse to gain as much truth as possible to better understand living the life of sacrifice. Today, we will focus on the very next verse that offers us even more insight into Paul's urging of how we should live in response to Jesus.

> DO NOT CONFORM TO THE PATTERN OF THIS WORLD, BUT BE TRANSFORMED BY THE RENEWING OF YOUR MIND. THEN YOU WILL BE ABLE TO TEST AND APPROVE WHAT GOD'S WILL IS—HIS GOOD, PLEASING AND PERFECT WILL.
>
> — ROMANS 12:2

Regardless of anyone's belief system, most people would likely agree that the world has always had clear patterns in place. While the lines today are continually shifting and blurred, the patterns stand firm. From politics and religion to matters of money and sex, we are given the parameters to which we are expected to conform.

As Paul often did in his teaching, verse 2 provides the new "don't and do" or the "stop and start." He encourages us to stop conforming to the world's mold. In our world, to step off the speeding assembly line of popular culture where everyone else is going with the flow. The new alternative is to allow God to renew and transform our minds. The renewal is an event upon salvation, but the transformation is an ongoing process of change.

When someone tells you that they will not be attending an event that you had planned together, once you hear the decision, the very next question is always: "*What* changed your mind?" or "*Why* did you change your mind?" Hearing the new choice—the what—is usually not enough for us, we want to know *why* the decision was made. Often processing the person's answer will determine whether our disappointment turns to frustration or understanding.

When we evaluate any behavior and decide to change, the determination occurs first in the mind. Yes, the heart will be involved, but the crucial turning point will be in the mind. But changing behavior first requires learning to think differently.

Some simple, everyday examples of this mental process are:

• If the milk is moved to a lower shelf of the refrigerator, it takes several times to stop looking in the old place.

• If your office is moved from the second floor to the fourth, it can take a few days to hit the right button on the elevator.

• If you move across town in a different direction, it can take a while to re-member to take the right road heading to the new home.

To change habits and patterns of any kind, we have to first reprogram the brain for the new location.

When we finally exchange one of the world's programmed patterns and start to think differently in any area of life because of our walk with Christ, what happens next?

Your new thinking leads to new behavior, which gives you your own personal experience with God's will. You personalize and customize his will in your life. The truth is no longer just a truth; it's *your* truth. You have proven its merit for yourself.

Jeremy Camp has spent years speaking and singing God's truth to millions of people because he had his own truth that was formed in his life as he had been *"able to test and approve what God's will is."*

Anyone can argue theology and debate matters of faith, but how does someone argue with your changed life? Dispute your personal experience? Question your own evidence of God's will? When we choose to renew rather than conform, we repent—do a 180-about-face, go in God's direction, and get off the world's assembly line.

ALTAR TO ACCOLADES

Considering everything we have discussed about Romans 12:1-3, let's take a look back in history for a great visual example of the total transformation of a life.

In medieval days, when a young man had successfully completed all the training to become a knight, he entered into a series of ceremonies to exemplify his commitment and transformation.

The Vigil: On his final night as a squire, he would go through a ritual bath to thoroughly wash his body as a symbol of purification. Afterward, he would go alone to the altar of a chapel or church and spend the night there in prayer. His sword and shield were laid on the altar where he would spend up to ten hours in prayer and meditation.

The Accolade: The next morning his counterparts and the clergy joined him where he would take his oaths of knighthood.

The Dubbing: Head bowed on his knees in submission to an elder knight, he would be "dubbed' by his sword, given a new title along with the authority of a knight.

The Celebration: A feast with a lot of fanfare would follow to conclude the knight's transformation to a new role and new way of life with new commitments and responsibilities.

From the all-night prayers to the honorable lifestyle to which the knight was now committed, these ceremonies were deeply rooted in Christian ideals. This is a powerful picture and metaphor of our commitment to a life of sacrifice and agreement to leave behind our old lives to enter into a new role and responsibility with a new way of thinking and living.

> "A lot of people have asked me, 'How in the world do you stand next to Jeremy while he's talking about another woman? For me, I don't see it that way. Because the truth is this whole thing is not about Melissa. And it's not about me. It's not about Jeremy. It really is about eternity and just lifting our eyes above the situation. It is about the greater good, a bigger purpose, and something that is so much bigger than ourselves. If I didn't sacrifice my preferences, maybe I wouldn't want to talk about this, but it's the sacrifice. The greater good."

ADRIENNE CAMP

getting personal

IDENTIFY A FEW "PATTERNS OF THIS WORLD" THAT YOU HAVE TO CONTEND WITH AT WORK, IN THE COMMUNITY, OR EVEN AT CHURCH.

WHAT ARE SOME "PATTERNS OF THIS WORLD" THAT YOU FEEL YOU ARE CONSTANTLY BATTLING TO OVERCOME?

WHAT IS ONE AREA IN YOUR LIFE WHERE YOU HAVE EXPERIENCED GOD'S TRANSFORMATION AND RENEWAL?

IF SOMEONE ASKED YOU FOR A TESTIMONY OF A TIME YOU HAD "TESTED AND APPROVED GOD'S WILL," WHAT WOULD YOU SHARE?

IF YOU DECIDED TO CREATE YOUR OWN VIGIL—AN ALL-NIGHT PRAYER RETREAT—WHAT WOULD YOU PRIORITIZE TO BRING BEFORE GOD?

WRITE IN THE BLANKS TO CREATE YOUR OWN CURRENT, CUSTOM VERSION OF ROMANS 12:1-3:

IN VIEW OF GOD'S MERCY, TODAY I OFFER TO SACRIFICE (A TEMPTATION OR ISSUE)

AS MY TRUE AND PROPER WORSHIP. TODAY, I WON'T CONFORM TO (A PATTERN YOU STRUGGLE WITH)

BUT I'LL BE TRANSFORMED BY (WHAT YOU ARE ASKING GOD TO DO)

TO TEST AND APPROVE WHAT GOD'S WILL IS—HIS GOOD, PLEASING, AND PERFECT WILL.

Day 5

THE PRESENCE IN PRAISE

One of the major features of Jeremy Camp's ministry has been to lead the body of Christ in worship all over the world through live events and his songs being sung in the church. The events of his life and his faith journey have forged a deep well from which he can draw to take people to the throne of God. That is our focus regarding sacrifice in our final day of study this week.

THE PRESENCE IN PRAISE

God created the people of every generation and every race to worship him. But with that innate desire to worship, as a result of sin, we can place our adoration, loyalty, and recognition in the wrong place—material things, personal status, other people, and even ourselves. Using the analogy from two days ago, we decide who or what will be placed on the throne of our lives, and all too often, the entrance can become a revolving door.

We began our study of sacrifice this week in Hebrews 12. Today, we close in Hebrews 13:15-16.

> THROUGH
> JESUS,
> THEREFORE,
> LET US
> CONTINUALLY
> OFFER TO GOD
> A SACRIFICE OF
> PRAISE—THE
> FRUIT OF
> LIPS THAT
> OPENLY

PROFESS HIS NAME. AND DO NOT FORGET TO DO
GOOD AND TO SHARE WITH OTHERS, FOR WITH SUCH
SACRIFICES GOD IS PLEASED.

In Matthew, Mark, and Luke, Jesus taught us that the greatest commandment
is to love God with all our hearts, souls, and minds, and then our neighbor as
ourselves. As sinners, placing God and others before our own needs and desires
requires sacrificing our will and ego. The writer of Hebrews encourages us
"through Jesus" to "continually offer to God a sacrifice of praise." If we are constantly choosing to give our praise to God alone, we will be able to fulfill Jesus's
singular commandment. Our lips produce fruit when we are testifying of the
good things of God.

In Jeremy and Adrienne Camp's interviews for the *I Still Believe* video lessons,
Jeremy shared a powerful testimony about one of the most difficult seasons of
his life that perfectly illustrates "the sacrifice of praise."

> **"One of the most powerful moments of me
> experiencing the presence of God was after Melissa
> died. I was on the floor just curled up in a fetal
> position, just devastated. And God spoke to my heart
> and said, 'Stand up and worship me.' I remember that
> moment of just kind of arguing with him, thinking, 'I
> don't feel like worshipping right now. That's the last
> thing I want to do.'**
>
> **"I finally was obedient—not because God was saying
> 'I demand your worship,' but it was a moment of Him
> saying, 'Trust me, stand and worship me.' So I stood
> up and worshipped, raised my hands, and in the
> whole room in that moment, there was worship. I felt**

> **a tangible sense of God's presence. If I wouldn't have done that and been obedient, I would've missed out on understanding that truth, as if he was saying, 'In the midst of your hardest time, I didn't leave you. I didn't forsake you. I was actually there that very moment. Could you feel me?' And I answered, 'Yeah, I felt you. You were there and very present in my time in need.'**
>
> **"When I didn't want to sacrifice, but then stood up and worshipped, God came through in the most beautiful time."**

JEREMY CAMP

When we "don't feel like worshipping right now" because that is "the last thing we want to do," yet we sacrifice our own will and feelings, crawl off the throne, and onto the altar, God can respond and surround us with his presence. This is a game-changer moment every time.

IS GOD COMFORTABLE HERE?

In our modern church culture, we can easily relegate worship to singing a few songs on Sunday morning. And so often, by the time we finally shake off the stress and struggles of the week, that allotted time in the service is over. In the Western church, most people tend to ask, "Am I comfortable here?" The better question would be, "Is God comfortable here?"

Worship is not really an earthly event we attend, but rather a Heavenly activity in which we take part in. Whether in our personal or corporate worship of God, we are attributing or ascribing worth to him and him alone. Regardless of the method or expression of praise like singing, lifting hands, sitting in reverent stillness, or bowing down, we are declaring who God is and at the same time whom anyone or anything else is not.

Worship helps us move our faith from our heads to our hearts. The connection occurs not just because we know about him but we know him! Love is best shown and experienced when it is not passive but active, when expressed, not repressed. For that reason, sacrificing our praise and giving worship to God is as much about our ongoing attitude as our expressions to him.

To sum up, worship is the outward expression of:
• An inward change
• Being in God's presence
• A total commitment

Praise is a(n):
• Acknowledgement of God's presence
• Response to receiving God's blessings
• Focusing in on who God is
• Focusing in on what he has done for us

"Nothing teaches us about the preciousness of the Creator as much as when we learn the emptiness of everything else."

—CHARLES SPURGEON

getting personal

WHY DO YOU SUPPOSE GOD DOESN'T FORCE OR DEMAND
OUR WORSHIP BUT SIMPLY OFFERS AN ONGOING INVITATION?

WHY DOES TRUE WORSHIP OF GOD REQUIRE A SACRIFICE OF
OUR SELVES?

WHAT STRUCK YOU THE MOST ABOUT JEREMY'S TESTIMONY?
WHY?

WHY DO YOU THINK ASKING "IS GOD COMFORTABLE HERE?" A
BETTER QUESTION THAN IF WE ARE COMFORTABLE?

DID ANY POINT TODAY EXPAND YOUR VIEW OF WORSHIP? IF SO, HOW?

WHAT IS YOUR GREATEST STRUGGLE REGARDING YOUR OWN PERSONAL WORSHIP?

WE WILL ALL EXPERIENCE THE SAME FEELINGS. JEREMY DID IN HIS SEASON OF GRIEF AS HE CONFESSED THAT WORSHIP WAS THE LAST THING HE WANTED TO DO. THE NEXT TIME YOU FEEL THIS WAY, CONSIDER GOING TO THE PSALMS AND READ THE WORDS OUT LOUD AS YOUR OWN. THIS IS BIBLICAL WORSHIP YOU CAN PERSONALIZE TO CONVEY YOUR CURRENT STATE OF MIND AND HEART. PASSAGES LIKE PSALM 28:6-7:

> PRAISE BE TO THE LORD,
>
>> FOR HE HAS HEARD MY CRY FOR MERCY.
>
> THE LORD IS MY STRENGTH AND MY SHIELD;
>
>> MY HEART TRUSTS IN HIM, AND HE HELPS ME.
>
> MY HEART LEAPS FOR JOY,
>
>> AND WITH MY SONG I PRAISE HIM.

Day 6

CALL TO ACTION

Your first five days have been fully focused on deepening and processing the study content. Today is all about forming a plan to apply and implement the truths you have taken in. So the sixth day of each week in this study is one of the most important to help you carry the truths you learn far past these five weeks to make them a permanent part of your walk with Christ.

Jesus continually invited his disciples to engage with him and experience his work for themselves. His goal was always for them to apply his truths because God's plan was for them to take over the spread of the Gospel after he returned to Heaven. God wants the same for you today as you carry out his will, ways, and work into the world. Remember James's words from this week: "Do not merely listen to the word, and so deceive yourselves. Do what it says." (James 1:22)

The goal of writing down your answers is solely to help you commit to being proactive toward anything God is calling you to do in obedience to him. May God grant you the grace and boldness to carry out what he calls you to do.

WHAT BIBLE VERSE OR PASSAGE DID YOU MOST CONNECT WITH THIS WEEK? NEXT, WRITE DOWN WHY YOU FEEL THAT MESSAGE CONNECTED AND THE IMPACT IT HAD ON YOU.

WHAT WAS ONE TRUTH OR PRINCIPLE YOU BELIEVE GOD SPOKE TO YOU THIS PAST WEEK?

HAS GOD IMPRESSED ANY NEW THING ON YOU THAT YOU BELIEVE HE WANTS YOU TO BEGIN?

HAS GOD IMPRESSED ANYTHING ON YOU THAT YOU BELIEVE HE WANTS YOU TO SURRENDER TO HIM?

THIS WEEK, WAS THERE ANY RELATIONSHIP IN YOUR LIFE THAT
YOU SENSED GOD WANTS YOU TO TAKE SOME SORT OF ACTION?

A CHRISTIAN FRIEND YOU NEED TO ENCOURAGE?

A NON-CHRISTIAN YOU NEED TO MINISTER TO?

GOD'S WILL

WHAT ARE SOME PRACTICAL STEPS YOU CAN TAKE TO
BE OBEDIENT TO WHAT GOD SHOWED YOU THIS WEEK?

GOD'S WILL

Day 7

PREP & PRAY

he following are instructions and encouragement for your seventh day of each of the five weeks. For the other seventh days in this Journal, only your review will be provided, but follow these tips on those important prep and pray days.

IF YOU ARE USING THIS JOURNAL IN CONNECTION WITH A SMALL GROUP STUDY ...

This should be the day of your small group meeting for the *I Still Believe* study. We want to give you the grace and space for two things:

1. If you need to catch up on any day that you may have missed, this time will allow you to be sure you engage fully with *all* the content. If you were pressed for time on any particular day, use this opportunity to go back and review.

2. We want to give you an opportunity to prepare for your group meeting so you can offer all you need to contribute.

In any small group, the real goal for every member is transformation, not information; for members to not just attend, but experience. Your place and contribution in your group is vital, so your interaction is crucial for the entire group to receive from you as you receive from them. Consider this: Something you say might be the very thing a member of your group needs to hear for their lives. God can use you to encourage someone by your availability and obedience. You are in your group for two reasons: to grow and to give.

Preparation for Your Small Group Meeting

LOOKING BACK OVER YOUR FIVE DAYS AND CALL TO ACTION,
WRITE DOWN YOUR ANSWERS TO THESE QUESTIONS.

DO YOU HAVE A QUESTION YOU WOULD WANT TO RAISE TO THE GROUP
LEADER FOR FURTHER CLARIFICATION OR DISCUSSION?

WAS THERE ANY CONTENT YOU STRUGGLED TO UNDERSTAND AND
WOULD LIKE TO HAVE CLARITY? (REMEMBER—GETTING YOUR QUESTION
ANSWERED COULD HELP SOMEONE ELSE.)

DID GOD SHOW YOU ANY TRUTH OR PRINCIPLE FROM THE STUDY THIS
WEEK THAT YOU FEEL YOU WOULD LIKE TO SHARE WITH THE GROUP?

CONSIDERING THE SPECIFIC SCRIPTURES FROM THIS WEEK, DID YOU HAVE A
QUESTION OR COMMENT YOU WOULD WANT TO SHARE WITH THE GROUP?

DID SOMETHING SIGNIFICANT HAPPEN IN YOUR WALK WITH GOD THIS
WEEK THAT YOU WOULD LIKE TO SHARE OR REQUEST PRAYER FOR?

HOW WOULD YOU SUM UP YOUR ENGAGEMENT WITH THE *I STILL
BELIEVE* STUDY THIS WEEK IN ONE OR TWO SENTENCES?

Pray for Your Small Group

Take a few minutes to pray for your group meeting. Pray for your leader, each member by name, and any requests where members have asked for prayer. Ask God to open your mind and heart to receive what he has for you and also for wisdom in what you need to contribute to your group's dynamic.

If you are using this Journal for your personal study only

Today allows you the opportunity to catch up on the content if needed. The questions below are designed to help you evaluate your experience this week, as well as indicate any area that you may need to seek out help or share with someone. Remember—don't be shy about going to a pastor, church leader, or trusted Christian friend if you realize you have a need.

LOOKING BACK OVER YOUR FIVE DAYS AND CALL TO ACTION,
WRITE DOWN YOUR ANSWERS TO THESE QUESTIONS.

DO YOU HAVE A BIBLICAL OR SPIRITUAL QUESTION
THAT YOU WOULD LIKE TO HAVE ANSWERED?

WAS THERE ANY CONTENT YOU STRUGGLED TO
UNDERSTAND AND WOULD LIKE TO HAVE CLARITY?

DID GOD SHOW YOU ANY TRUTH OR PRINCIPLE FROM THE STUDY THIS WEEK
THAT YOU FEEL YOU NEED TO SHARE WITH SOMEONE IN YOUR LIFE? WHO?

CONSIDERING THE SPECIFIC SCRIPTURES FROM THIS WEEK, DID YOU
HAVE A QUESTION YOU NEED ANSWERED OR SOMETHING YOU FEEL
YOU SHOULD SHARE WITH SOMEONE?

DID SOMETHING SIGNIFICANT HAPPEN IN YOUR WALK WITH GOD THIS
WEEK THAT YOU FEEL YOU NEED TO SHARE WITH SOMEONE AND/OR
ASK THAT PERSON TO PRAY WITH YOU?

HOW WOULD YOU SUM UP YOUR ENGAGEMENT WITH THE
I STILL BELIEVE STUDY THIS WEEK IN ONE OR TWO SENTENCES?

Prayer Time

Take a few minutes to pray for yourself and anyone that God brought to your heart
this week or today in your evaluation. Ask God to open your mind and heart to
receive what he has for you and also for wisdom in any actions you need to take.

WRITE YOUR PRAYER HERE

father,

2

YOU ARE
FAITHFUL

Redemption

Day 8

CHRIST'S OFFER, YOUR CHOICE

From the day Jeremy Camp left home with his brand new guitar to start a fresh chapter of life and adventure at college in California, God's story of faithfulness was put into motion. From the first frame of *I Still Believe*, God's story of redemption unfolds to show us both the beauty and battle of belief.

For the person who surrenders to Christ, that same story of faithfulness and redemption begins. The details of our lives are always as unique and personally customized as our fingerprints, but the overarching theme of God's promises is the foundation of every redeemed life.

CHRIST'S OFFER, YOUR CHOICE

BUT GLORY, HONOR AND PEACE
FOR EVERYONE WHO DOES
GOOD: FIRST FOR THE JEW, THEN
FOR THE GENTILE. FOR GOD DOES
NOT SHOW FAVORITISM.

- ROMANS 2:10-11

When some people look at the life of a successful Christian artist, it might be easy to make assumptions: "Well, of course, God worked everything out in the end for Jeremy Camp. He sings worship songs and shares the Gospel all over the world. But I will never have that kind of platform or opportunity, so I will never have a story like that."

The first person to shoot this thinking down would be Jeremy himself. Jeremy's favor is not because of what he *does*. He has simply responded in obedience to what God has given him. He responded to the calling. Jeremy's favor is *because* of his relationship with Jesus Christ. One of the major goals of *I Still Believe*, from the song to the film to this Journal, is to clearly state that God's faithfulness and redemption is one hundred percent available to everyone—to you.

AS SCRIPTURE SAYS, "ANYONE WHO BELIEVES IN HIM WILL NEVER BE PUT TO SHAME." FOR THERE IS NO DIFFERENCE BETWEEN JEW AND GENTILE—THE SAME LORD IS LORD OF ALL AND RICHLY BLESSES ALL WHO CALL ON HIM, FOR, "EVERYONE WHO CALLS ON THE NAME OF THE LORD WILL BE SAVED."

- ROMANS 10:11-13

With this truth in mind, the difference then lies in the choice of what a person does in their relationship with Christ. Consider this analogy:

You and a friend decide to fly to a destination several hours away. You buy seats next to one another in first class. As you settle in and buckle up, the flight attendant asks you both, "Can I get you something to drink?" Your friend places an order, but you say no. The flight attendant returns and asks if you would like the complimentary meal. Your friend says yes but you say no. In-flight movie with earbuds streamed to your individual screen? Friend says yes; you say no. Blanket? Pillow? Hot towel? Every time your friend accepts and you say no.

You both had your tickets. You were on the same flight and seated in the same section. You will arrive together at the same destination. You had all the same amenities offered with the price already paid.

The only difference in experience was the answers given to the offers made.

Once anyone comes to Christ, yes, circumstances can create a wide range of starting points. But Christ offers all of himself to every follower and disciple. The beauty of the Gospel is that nothing is withheld from anyone for any reason. There is an old saying:

The ground is level at the foot of the cross.

in this reality from day one. But so many people will allow a painful past, poor self-esteem, or personal dysfunction to hinder the opportunities that Christ makes available. If you gain only one truth from this Journal, please know and accept that the Gospel is for *you* and *nothing* is withheld from you in God's kingdom. Because of Christ, you are an adopted son or daughter of the King of kings and Lord of lords! The thought is so humbling but as real as the air you breathe.

HE MAKES ALL THINGS NEW

Taking in the above Scriptures and thoughts, Christ offers us a:

• New Place to Look

Week in and week out, we all have bills to pay, problems to solve, and people demanding our attention. Physically, we are looking at the same world everyone else sees. But a relationship with Jesus allows us to take our eyes off the stuff of the world to look at his hope, his kingdom, his faithfulness, and the redemption he will ultimately bring to pass. For the Christ-follower, the best is *always* yet to come—here or Heaven.

> I KEEP MY EYES ALWAYS ON
> THE LORD. WITH HIM AT MY RIGHT
> HAND, I WILL NOT BE SHAKEN.
>
> - PSALM 16:8

• New Way to Think

The thoughts, attitudes, and motives of our minds are often either our greatest enemy or our strongest ally. *How* we think and *what* we think will always determine what we *do* and who we *become*. Paul tells us in Romans 12 that Christ can renew and transform our minds. His redemption can create a positive, optimistic, "glass-half-full" mindset. Inside our critical culture, an attitude focused on Christ's faithfulness will allow us to not only be healthier people but also draw others to him.

SET YOUR MINDS ON THINGS ABOVE, NOT ON EARTHLY THINGS.

- COLOSSIANS 3:2

• New Life to Live

Jesus offers us the abundant life he describes in John 10. The offer stands, but the choice is ours. New life in Christ is not only a *different* way to live but also the *best* way to live.

I HAVE COME THAT THEY MAY HAVE LIFE, AND HAVE IT TO THE FULL.

- JOHN 10:10

"Jesus said, 'I'm the way, I'm the truth. I'm the life. No man comes to the father except through me.' I'm thankful that he saved a wretch like me and gave me a new life. And then we're able to go out and proclaim his goodness, his redemption, and tell people that they have a purpose and a plan that God has in store. Trust him in every step. He'll lead you and direct you."

JEREMY CAMP

getting personal

WHY DO YOU SUPPOSE SO MANY CHRISTIANS, AS WELL AS NON-BELIEVERS, LOOK AT A BLESSED PERSON'S LIFE AND THINK GOD WILL NOT DO THE SAME FOR THEM, EVEN AFTER READING SCRIPTURES LIKE ROMANS 2:10-11?

CONSIDER THE STATEMENT: "THE DETAILS OF OUR LIVES ARE ALWAYS AS UNIQUE AND PERSONALLY CUSTOMIZED AS OUR FINGERPRINTS, BUT THE OVERARCHING THEME OF GOD'S PROMISES IS THE FOUNDATION OF EVERY REDEEMED LIFE." HOW DOES THIS TRUTH ENCOURAGE YOU TO REMOVE ANY EXCUSES FOR BELIEVING WHAT GOD CAN DO IN YOUR LIFE?

WHAT ARE YOUR THOUGHTS ON THE FIRST-CLASS FLIGHT ANALOGY, PARTICULARLY THE CLOSING STATEMENT: "THE ONLY DIFFERENCE IN EXPERIENCE WAS THE ANSWERS GIVEN TO THE OFFERS MADE"?

IN YOUR RELATIONSHIP WITH CHRIST, IS THERE AN ADJUSTMENT YOU NEED TO MAKE IN YOUR "NEW PLACE TO LOOK"—WHERE YOU TEND TO FOCUS?

IN YOUR RELATIONSHIP WITH CHRIST, IS THERE AN ADJUSTMENT YOU NEED TO MAKE IN YOUR "NEW WAY TO THINK"—YOUR THOUGHT PROCESS?

IN YOUR RELATIONSHIP WITH CHRIST, IS THERE AN ADJUSTMENT YOU NEED TO MAKE IN YOUR "NEW LIFE TO LIVE"—BELIEVING IN WHAT ONLY GOD CAN DO IN YOU?

IF JESUS CAME TO YOU TODAY AND REMINDED YOU THAT HE HAS GIVEN YOU ALL OF HIMSELF, IS THERE ANYTHING YOU WOULD STILL WANT TO ASK OF HIM? EXPLAIN.

Day 9

THE GOSPEL ACCORDING TO EDITH

Edith always introduced herself by saying, "Hello, my name is Edith Burns. Do you believe in Easter?" Then she would explain the biblical story of Christ's death and resurrection. Often, people would pray with her to receive Christ.

Edith was Doctor Will Phillips's favorite patient. After a series of tests, he delivered the report to her, "You have cancer and you're not going to live very long." Edith responded, "Why are you so sad? You just told me I'm going to see my precious Lord Jesus, my husband, and my friends. I am going to celebrate Easter forever, and here you are having difficulty giving me my ticket!"

A few months later, Edith called Dr. Phillips from the hospital. "Will, I'm very near home, so would you make sure that they put women in my room who need to know about Easter?" The doctor agreed, and as a result, many women came to know Christ. From the staff to patients, everyone began to call her "Edith Easter."

Everyone loved Edith except the head nurse, Phyllis Cross. Phyllis, a tough ex-Army nurse, thought Edith was just a "religious nut." One morning, Edith needed a shot, but no other nurses were available. Edith smiled and said, "Phyllis, God loves you and I love you. I have been praying for you." Nurse Cross snapped, "Well, you can quit praying for me. I'm not interested." Edith continued, "I have asked God not to let me go home until you come into his family." Phyllis quipped, "Then you will never die, because that will never happen," and stormed out of the room.

Several days later, Phyllis said she was strangely drawn into Edith's room and sat down on her bed. Edith said, "I'm so glad you have come because God told me that today is your special day." Phyllis asked, "Edith, you have asked everybody here the question, 'Do you believe in Easter?' but you have never asked me." Edith responded, "Phyllis, I wanted to many times, but God told me to wait until you asked me first, so now that you have …"

Edith proceeded to take her Bible and share with Phyllis about the death, burial, and resurrection of Jesus. Edith then asked, "Do you believe that Jesus is alive and that he wants to live in your heart?" Phyllis answered, "I want to believe that with all my heart, and I do want Jesus in my life." Right there, Edith led Phyllis in prayer and invited Christ into her heart.

Four days later was Easter Sunday, Phyllis came into work, bringing lilies for Edith. When she walked into the room, Edith's eyes were closed, a sweet smile on her face, and her Bible open. Phyllis realized Edith had passed with her left hand holding open the page with John 14:2-3 marked. Her right hand was holding open the page with Revelation 21:4 marked. Phyllis lifted her face toward Heaven, tears streaming down her cheeks, and said, "Happy Easter, Edith, Happy Easter!"

She walked out of the room, over to a table where two student nurses were sitting, and said, "Hi, my name is Phyllis Cross. Do you believe in Easter?"

Edith's left hand was marking John 14:2-4:

"MY FATHER'S HOUSE HAS MANY ROOMS; IF THAT WERE NOT SO, WOULD I HAVE TOLD YOU THAT I AM GOING THERE TO PREPARE A PLACE FOR YOU? AND IF I GO AND PREPARE A PLACE FOR YOU, I WILL COME BACK AND TAKE YOU TO BE WITH ME THAT YOU ALSO MAY BE WHERE I AM."

Her left hand was marking Revelation 21:4:

"HE WILL WIPE EVERY TEAR FROM THEIR EYES. THERE WILL BE NO MORE DEATH' OR MOURNING OR CRYING OR PAIN, FOR THE OLD ORDER OF THINGS HAS PASSED AWAY."

"Redemption comes like a breath of fresh air. This is the gospel message. How Jesus redeemed all mankind from the state of sin and depravity. All humans try to get to God but fail and fall. The whole redemption story is how Jesus took our place to be the ultimate sacrifice and redeem all mankind. So there's going to be a day where there's no more tears, no more sorrow, no more pain. It's what we look forward to, but we have to always remember the cost. That's why the scars on Jesus's wrists are still there to say, 'This is what I paid for you. It's a reminder of what I went through as the sacrifice. But it's beautiful.'"

JEREMY CAMP

MANY MESSENGERS, SAME MESSAGE

Jeremy Camp has spent the past twenty years sharing the same story as Edith Burns. His songs have reached people he will never see. His family has sacrificed as he has traveled the world to share the Gospel. Jeremy, Adrienne, and their children have taken the responsibility and stewardship to share the Gospel very seriously. So did Edith Burns as she shared with people every-where she went. But the same should be true for every person who receives the Gospel. Certainly, there are those who are amazingly gifted to share the Gospel in a unique way, but we are all stewards of the message of Christ.

In 2 Corinthians 5:17-19, Paul did not offer a suggestion to believers, but rather a command for the days we remain on the earth:

> THEREFORE, IF ANYONE IS IN CHRIST, THE NEW
> CREATION HAS COME: THE OLD HAS GONE, THE NEW IS
> HERE! ALL THIS IS FROM GOD, WHO RECONCILED US TO
> HIMSELF THROUGH CHRIST AND GAVE US THE MINISTRY
> OF RECONCILIATION: THAT GOD WAS RECONCILING THE
> WORLD TO HIMSELF IN CHRIST, NOT COUNTING PEOPLE'S
> SINS AGAINST THEM. AND HE HAS COMMITTED TO US THE
> MESSAGE OF RECONCILIATION.

Have you ever thought about why God leaves us here in this fallen world after we have accepted Christ and can go to Heaven? Because he is God, he could take us up whenever he wants. But he does not leave us here just to wait on our name to be called. He has a plan and a purpose for us to share his story of redemption—the story of Easter—with our circles of influence. There are people in your life right now that you are the very best person to reach them in the unique way you would share the Gospel. Not Jeremy Camp, your priest, or your pastor, but you! ☐

getting personal

WHY DO YOU SUPPOSE EDITH BURNS ALWAYS STARTED HER GOSPEL CONVERSATION ASKING ABOUT EASTER? HOW DID THAT APPROACH HELP HER IN SHARING?

WHAT DO YOU THINK CAUSES SO MANY CHRISTIANS TO BE AFRAID OF SHARING THE GOSPEL WITH OTHERS?

IS THERE ANYTHING THAT CAUSES YOU TO BE FEARFUL OR BECOMES A HINDRANCE IN SHARING THE GOSPEL? EXPLAIN.

WHY IS THE APPROACH THAT SOMEONE TAKES IN SHARING THE GOSPEL JUST AS IMPORTANT AS GETTING THE MESSAGE RIGHT?

WHY SHOULD WE VIEW PAUL'S WORDS IN 2 CORINTHIANS 5:17-19 AS A COMMAND AND NOT JUST A SUGGESTION?

TAKE A FEW MINUTES AND WRITE THE NAMES OF PEOPLE IN YOUR VARIOUS CIRCLES THAT YOU KNOW NEED CHRIST AS WELL AS THOSE YOU MAY BE UNCERTAIN ABOUT.

OVER THE NEXT FEW WEEKS, PRAY FOR THOSE ON YOUR LIST AND WATCH FOR OPPORTUNITIES OR OPENINGS IN CONVERSATIONS TO SHARE YOUR FAITH. REMEMBER—NO ONE CAN ARGUE WITH A CHANGED LIFE, SO SHARE YOUR STORY OF WHAT CHRIST HAS DONE FOR YOU.

Day 10

I CAN'T IMAGINE LIFE WITHOUT YOU

Jeremy Camp shares: "One of the most beautiful parts of our story is how I have had the opportunity to share what God did, sharing how he's been so faithful and proclaiming his goodness in front of literally thousands upon thousands of people. I've been able to tell them, 'I *still* believe in God's faithfulness because he *has been* so faithful.'

"And then I have also been able to share the beautiful thing that happened when Adrienne and I met. I had walked off the stage, and she came up to say she heard me talk about Melissa. She told me how Melissa's story ministered to her heart, and she was *that one* that Melissa had talked about that would make the sacrifice worth it. We got to see the redeeming factor of Adrienne and I meeting and how God had used me sharing about his faithfulness to impact Adrienne.

"Another beautiful picture of God's redemption happened years later when my daughter Bella said to me, 'Dad, I've been praying for something, and God hasn't answered my prayer.' So to help her understand, I explained that there are times when God just keeps telling us to press into him and trust. Sometimes he does say no, sometimes wait. But then I reminded her about Melissa and how if God had healed her like I wanted, then I wouldn't have met and married her mom and then she wouldn't be here. I told Bella how I couldn't imagine life without her and how she is such a beautiful picture of God's redemption. My children are signs of God's faithfulness in my life. That was really a special, sweet moment. But those blessings don't come without a cost."

KEEP MOVING FORWARD

On July 23, 2003, just four months into the war in Iraq, a Humvee was leading a convoy of soldiers between Ar Ramadi and Fallujah when an IED, a hidden bomb in the road, exploded as the vehicle rolled over it. As the blast ripped through the armor, Captain Josh Byers, just 29 years old, called out, "Sergeant, we've hit an IED. Keep moving forward."

The sergeant hit the gas, and the vehicle rolled on, but soon came to a stop from the damage. Investigators said that by not stopping at the moment of the blast at least two lives were saved. But ironically, as the smoke cleared, the other soldiers realized Captain Byers was dead. No one is certain how he was able to calmly but firmly call out the order to "keep moving forward" when he was mortally wounded and died within seconds.

Captain Byers was known by all who worked with him to be a strong man of God who was very open about his faith in Jesus Christ. General Charles "Hondo" Campbell said of Byers, "As a soldier and a leader, Josh was others-focused, a servant-leader, and a Christian soldier."

Terrorists may have taken the life of this young Christ-follower, but because of the way he lived, they could never win. His life was marked and changed by Christ, so death had no victory. The testimony of his life will forever be his legacy.

To honor their son's service and sacrifice, Josh's parents, Lloyd and Mary Byers, started a foundation in Josh's memory to support soldiers' families that deal with PTSD and other struggles that come from losing a child or sibling so tragically and so young. Mary served as president of American Gold Star Mothers, a national organization that supports moms who have lost children in service. As Christians with a long history of ministry, they would have never been involved in serving so many parents in the United States had their son not sacrificed his life for his country and his fellow soldiers.

As Jeremy stated, "But those blessings don't come without a cost."

When God had the idea of us and fashioned us in our mother's wombs, as Psalm 143 says, he fitted us for eternity. Our spirits placed inside our bodies and minds will never die. The only question will be where they will go for eternity after this life.

WHEN THE PERISHABLE HAS BEEN CLOTHED WITH THE IMPERISHABLE, AND THE MORTAL WITH IMMORTALITY, THEN THE SAYING THAT IS WRITTEN WILL COME TRUE: "DEATH HAS BEEN SWALLOWED UP IN VICTORY." "WHERE, O DEATH, IS YOUR VICTORY? WHERE, O DEATH, IS YOUR STING?" THE STING OF DEATH IS SIN, AND THE POWER OF SIN IS THE LAW.

— 1 CORINTHIANS 15:54-56

OUR SPIRITS PLACED INSIDE OUR BODIES WILL NEVER DIE. THE ONLY QUESTION, WHERE WILL THEY GO FOR ETERNITY?

The ultimate end of God's faithfulness and his final redemption for Christ-followers is when we leave this earth to enter Heaven. Flesh, sin, and all our pain and problems will not accompany us there. When the perishable and the mortal pass on, death has no victory or sting because of Jesus. We will experience the glorification and perfection of our spirits finally becoming all we were created to be without sin. After we pass through death, we will get to see who we truly are.

While verses 54-56 are about eternity, verses 57-58 give us hope while we wait on Heaven.

> BUT THANKS BE TO GOD! HE GIVES US THE VICTORY THROUGH OUR LORD JESUS CHRIST. THEREFORE, MY DEAR BROTHERS AND SISTERS, STAND FIRM. LET NOTHING MOVE YOU. ALWAYS GIVE YOURSELVES FULLY TO THE WORK OF THE LORD, BECAUSE YOU KNOW THAT YOUR LABOR IN THE LORD IS NOT IN VAIN.
>
> — 1 CORINTHIANS 15:57-58

The soldiers reported Captain Byers' final words were to "keep moving forward." Paul gave the same type of encouragement to the Corinthians and to us: "Stand firm. Let nothing move you." The bottom line—because of Jesus, let *nothing* stop you.

keep moving forward

getting personal

IN JEREMY'S TESTIMONY, HOW DO YOU SEE GOD'S REDEMPTION BROUGHT ABOUT BY HIS OBEDIENCE?

HOW WERE JEREMY'S CHILDREN A VERY REAL RESULT OF GOD SHOWING HIS FAITHFULNESS AND REDEMPTION?

IN THE STORY OF CAPTAIN BYERS, HOW DID HIS STRONG CHRISTIAN FAITH BRING AN ENTIRELY DIFFERENT DYNAMIC TO HIS HEROISM?

HOW DOES THE ETERNAL TRUTH OF 1 CORINTHIANS 15:54-56 ENCOURAGE US TODAY IN THE TEMPORARY REALM AS WE TRY TO LIVE OUT VERSES 57-58?

DO YOU HAVE A TESTIMONY OF HOW GOD TOOK A TRAGIC EVENT AND USED THE CIRCUMSTANCES TO SHOW YOU HIS REDEMPTION? WRITE DOWN THE STORY AS A SPIRITUAL MARKER FOR YOU TO REMEMBER.

USING THE PERSONALIZED WORDS OF 1 CORINTHIANS 15:57-58, PRAY THESE FOR YOUR DAY:

"BUT THANKS BE TO GOD! YOU GIVE ME THE VICTORY THROUGH MY LORD JESUS CHRIST. THEREFORE, HELP ME TO STAND FIRM. MAY NOTHING MOVE ME. STRENGTHEN ME TO ALWAYS GIVE MYSELF FULLY TO YOUR WORK, LORD, BECAUSE I KNOW THAT MY LABOR IN YOU IS NOT IN VAIN."

Day 11

THE INVESTMENT OF BELIEF

With access to who God is, in and through a relationship with Christ, we have the opportunity to take on his characteristics and qualities through his spirit. Certainly, a non-believer can display behavior such as love, kindness, goodness, and faithfulness in their actions. But God's Spirit provides a supernatural aspect to these and much more as we allow his life to be expressed through us for his glory, not our own.

Let's take a look at faithfulness from this perspective, but first, let's offer a simple, biblical definition: Faithfulness is expressing the loyalty of Jesus.

As we read the stories in the Old Testament, we see God's fierce faithfulness to his people. Even in times when he was displeased with their choices, he never abandoned them. In seasons where his people could not see his hand, we read the upper story to see how he was working on their behalf. Throughout the Gospels, we see Jesus's unwavering loyalty to his Father. He exhibited faithfulness to God's plan one hundred percent of the time. Faithfulness is also described throughout Jesus's teaching as a valued and respected quality.

In Matthew 25, Jesus tells a parable about a man going on a journey who called three of his servants to entrust his wealth to them while he was gone. The first man got five bags of gold, the second two bags, and the third one bag. The man with five bags of gold put his money to work and gained five more. The one with two bags of gold gained two more. But the man who received one bag went, dug a hole in the ground, and hid his master's money.

When the master returned, the man who had received five bags of gold brought the other five. Verse 21 says:

> "HIS MASTER REPLIED, 'WELL DONE, GOOD AND FAITHFUL SERVANT! YOU HAVE BEEN FAITHFUL WITH A FEW THINGS; I WILL PUT YOU IN CHARGE OF MANY THINGS. COME AND SHARE YOUR MASTER'S HAPPINESS!"

The man with two bags of gold brought his original two bags of gold with the two he had gained. Verse 23 says:

> "HIS MASTER REPLIED, 'WELL DONE, GOOD AND FAITHFUL SERVANT! YOU HAVE BEEN FAITHFUL WITH A FEW THINGS; I WILL PUT YOU IN CHARGE OF MANY THINGS. COME AND SHARE YOUR MASTER'S HAPPINESS!"

Then the man who had received one bag of gold came.

> 'MASTER,' HE SAID, 'I KNEW THAT YOU ARE A HARD MAN, HARVESTING WHERE YOU HAVE NOT SOWN AND GATHERING WHERE YOU HAVE NOT SCATTERED SEED. SO I WAS AFRAID AND WENT OUT AND HID YOUR GOLD IN THE GROUND. SEE, HERE IS WHAT BELONGS TO YOU.' "HIS MASTER REPLIED, 'YOU WICKED, LAZY SERVANT! SO YOU KNEW THAT I HARVEST WHERE I HAVE NOT SOWN AND GATHER WHERE I HAVE NOT SCATTERED SEED? WELL THEN, YOU SHOULD HAVE PUT MY MONEY ON DEPOSIT WITH THE BANKERS, SO THAT WHEN I RETURNED I WOULD HAVE RECEIVED IT BACK WITH INTEREST. "'SO TAKE THE BAG OF GOLD FROM HIM AND GIVE IT TO THE ONE WHO HAS TEN BAGS. FOR WHOEVER HAS WILL BE GIVEN MORE, AND THEY WILL HAVE AN ABUNDANCE. WHOEVER DOES NOT HAVE, EVEN WHAT THEY HAVE WILL BE TAKEN FROM THEM.

> —MATTHEW 25:24-29

Jesus's parable is not about the proper investment of money, but about being *faithful* to steward everything he gives us between salvation and Heaven. Whether this passage is interpreted as what we do with the Gospel or God's will in our lives overall, both are true and applicable. Gold and money will not go to Heaven, but our relationships will, along with how we have impacted people in Jesus's name.

WHEN WE GET TO HEAVEN, IT'S DONE

Our response to God's faithfulness can be expressed in two ways:

> 1. Our relationship with him

Remaining faithful to him, his Word, his will, and his principles throughout our lives is a journey few will choose to take, but we must.

> 2. Our relationships with others

From marriage to parenting to all our concentric circles of influence, being known as a reliable, trustworthy, and loyal person that keeps his/her promises is not only an amazing witness for Christ but also the best way to live.

We know that we can accept God's Word without question because of his faithfulness. Our goal is for him to know us as someone whose word can be accepted without question as well.

William Booth, the man who founded The Salvation Army, was once asked about its success:

"I will tell you the secret: God has had all that there was of me. There have been men with greater brains than I, even with greater opportunities, but from the day I got the poor of London on my heart and caught a vision of what Jesus Christ could do with me and them, on that day I made up my mind that God should have all of William Booth there was. And if there is anything of power in the Salvation Army, it is because God has had all the adoration of my heart, all the power of my will, and all the influence of my life."

"As much as we can get caught up in our lives here on earth, we have to remember that we're living for eternity, living for where there's no more tears and no more pain. All our struggles will be gone. Sin will be gone. The weight of everything in life will be gone. So the only time that we have to cling to the Lord is in the way we can here through trials. We're not going to have the testing of our faith in Heaven. This is the time for us to experience refinement and holding onto Jesus with everything we have. Because when we get to Heaven, it's done."

ADRIENNE CAMP

getting personal

WHAT ARE SOME DIFFERENCES YOU SEE BETWEEN THE WORLD'S VERSION OF FAITHFULNESS AND GOD'S?

WHAT ARE THE COMMON THREADS YOU SEE BETWEEN GOD'S FAITHFULNESS TO HIS PEOPLE IN THE OLD TESTAMENT AND JESUS TO HIS DISCIPLES IN THE NEW TESTAMENT?

IN JESUS'S PARABLE, WHY DO YOU SUPPOSE HE GAVE AN EXAMPLE OF EACH MAN GETTING DIFFERENT AMOUNTS RATHER THAN GIVING THEM ALL THE SAME?

HOW WAS THE THIRD MAN'S ATTITUDE THAT HE EXPRESSED TOWARD THE MASTER REFLECTED IN HIS INVESTMENT?

WHAT DO YOU THINK GOD MIGHT BE SPEAKING TO YOU TODAY IN JESUS'S PARABLE?

HOW MIGHT THE FINALITY OF ADRIENNE CAMP'S STATEMENT— "BECAUSE WHEN WE GET TO HEAVEN, IT'S DONE."—ENCOURAGE YOU TO GROW IN YOUR UNDERSTANDING AND EXPRESSION OF GOD'S FAITHFULNESS?

Day 12

A MASSIVE TRANSFORMATION

Adrienne Camp was asked to share her story of God's faithfulness and redemption of her life in her own words:

"When I think about the Gospel message, I honestly think about what my life was like before Christ. I grew up in a Christian home and had been very familiar with Jesus my whole life and always loved him. But then I reached what became such a defining moment of void, of my own emptiness.

"I was on the verge of making some of the most heinous and terrible mistakes of my life. And I literally felt like the Lord woke me up one day and said, 'This is not what I have for you.' I remember at that point falling on my knees, crying out to the Lord, and confessing, 'God, I need you. I'm so sick without you.' I knew I had missed the mark. I was so far from it.

"I remember praying, 'God, give me a love for people. Give me a love for your Word because the Bible means nothing to me right now.

Change my heart, come into my heart, and just change me.'

"There was such a massive transformation that took place in my life as I continued to seek the Lord. So many things began to change in me, the way that I thought through things. As I read Scripture, my mind was changed and renewed.

"Today, I'm still so hungry for that. I don't think we ever need to stop praying those prayers. It's important for us to come to the place where we surrender our entire life to Christ, invite him in. We need to do that all the time and just stay hungry."

The Christian life is not a religion or an event, but an ongoing, everyday relationship. Adrienne's challenge is exactly what God desires for us: to stay as hungry and desperate for him as the day we realized our need for him and prayed to invite him in.

Maybe you have a testimony like Adrienne, and as an adult came to the end of yourself and reached up for him. But because we live in a "Christian nation," when it comes to sharing their testimony, so many people will say things like: "I grew up in the church so I've always believed," or "I've just always known Jesus." The crucial detail is not *when* you came to Christ, but that you *know* you have come to Christ. For this reason, many adults find themselves questioning their faith because they were told they made a decision as a child but struggle to remember what happened.

If you should have any doubt whatsoever about your own salvation, regardless of when or how it came, God wants you to be certain and confident. Like Adrienne, should anyone ask you, you know your story and can share what happened. Good practice for this is writing out your testimony of your conversion to Christ. That is always a great marker. So if you struggle at all in writing out your story, get your relationship settled today. Don't wait. Go back and read Adrienne's story. Simply do what she did—surrender.

THE TWO SIDES OF THE CROSS

One of the most amazing stories of God's redemption in the entire Bible occurred while Jesus was at his peak of suffering on the cross. In this account, we see the two decisions people throughout the generations need to make, manifested in the men hanging on each side of Jesus.

> ONE OF THE CRIMINALS WHO HUNG THERE HURLED INSULTS AT HIM: "AREN'T YOU THE MESSIAH? SAVE YOURSELF AND US!" BUT THE OTHER CRIMINAL REBUKED HIM. "DON'T YOU FEAR GOD," HE SAID, "SINCE YOU ARE UNDER THE SAME SENTENCE? WE ARE PUNISHED JUSTLY, FOR WE ARE GETTING WHAT OUR DEEDS DESERVE. BUT THIS MAN HAS DONE NOTHING WRONG."

> —LUKE 23:39-41

Christ is on the cross, innocent of all sin, hanging between two thieves. Both are guilty, but their response to their sin is worlds apart.

Every human being has one of two responses regarding Jesus:

- Against or Accept
- Reject or Receive
- Self-centered or God-focused

But Christ, hanging on the cross in between the two extremes, died for *both*, making the choice available to *all* sinners.

The first man was full of anger and bitterness, threatening and mocking in disbelief. We hear this same voice screaming throughout our culture today, as loudly as ever.

The second man was remorseful and repentant, confessing his guilt his words were in defense of Jesus as well as Jesus's innocence. But the second criminal's final words are some of the most humbling and intriguing in all of Scripture.

THEN HE SAID, "JESUS, REMEMBER ME WHEN YOU COME INTO YOUR KINGDOM." JESUS ANSWERED HIM, "TRULY I TELL YOU, TODAY YOU WILL BE WITH ME IN PARADISE."

—LUKE 23:42-43

He called Jesus by name, expressing faith by stating he knew Christ would be returning to Heaven. But notice that the second thief didn't actually ask for salvation. He didn't say, "Save me," but "Remember me." His great guilt and realization of who Christ is caused him to think salvation was too far outside of the realm of possibilities. His words, in reality, meant, "Jesus, please don't forget about me, wherever I'm going." But Jesus knew the man's heart, saying in essence, "Not only will I remember you but this day you will be with me!"

Imagine for a moment what that man must have felt in his heart when he heard those words? Imagine for a moment suffering a terrifying and painful death, gasping to take another breath, and hearing the Son of God tell you that very day you will be with him in Paradise.

In contrast, Jesus never responded to the first thief's scornful insults. He only responded to the one who expressed faith. Even while dying on the cross, Jesus allowed the freedom to choose him or not.

What we can take away from this miraculous account of the cross is without full surrender, as in the case of the first thief, salvation will never occur. To God, the intent of the heart is more important than the choice of words. There is no magic formula to say, only a merciful Father to listen. ■

WITH FULL SURRENDER

AND PURE INTENT OF

THE HEART WE WILL FIND

salvation.

---

getting personal

WHY DO YOU SUPPOSE SO MANY PEOPLE'S TESTIMONIES INCLUDE A LOW POINT IN LIFE? WHAT IS THE CONNECTION OF THAT PARTICULAR STATE OF THE HEART TO FULL SURRENDER?

SHARE YOUR THOUGHTS ABOUT THIS STATEMENT: "ADRIENNE'S CHALLENGE IS EXACTLY WHAT GOD DESIRES FOR US: TO STAY AS HUNGRY AND DESPERATE FOR HIM AS THE DAY WE REALIZED OUR NEED FOR HIM AND PRAYED TO INVITE HIM IN."

WHAT ARE THE *STRUGGLES* THAT CAN COME AS AN ADULT FROM THOSE WHO HAD A CHILDHOOD SALVATION EXPERIENCE?

WHAT ARE THE *BLESSINGS* THAT CAN COME AS AN ADULT FROM
THOSE WHO HAD A CHILDHOOD SALVATION EXPERIENCE?

WHAT FEELINGS OR THOUGHTS DID YOU HAVE ABOUT
JESUS'S RESPONSE TO THE SECOND THIEF WHO ASKED TO BE
REMEMBERED?

EXERCISE

Take a few minutes to finish the following statements and reflect on how God is inviting you to deeper intimacy with him.

JESUS, I KNOW I HAVE A RELATIONSHIP WITH YOU TODAY BECAUSE:

FATHER, I KNOW YOU ARE FAITHFUL BECAUSE:

GREAT REDEEMER, I WORSHIP YOU TODAY BECAUSE:

PRAYER

Take a few minutes to write out a prayer asking God to change your heart and desires for him and his word.

Day 13

CALL TO ACTION

These past five days have been fully focused on deepening and processing the study content. Today is all about forming a plan to apply and implement the truths you have taken in. This sixth day is one of the most important to help you carry the truths you learn far past these five weeks to make them a permanent part of your walk with Christ.

Jesus always led his disciples by show-and-tell, not tell-and-go. He consistently invited his followers inside to become a part of what he was doing. Think for a moment about how many instances in the Gospels where he involved people in his work. Here are seven examples in only eight chapters in Matthew:

• Jesus sent his disciples out with the authority to heal and drive out demons. (10:1)
• He involved his disciples in the feeding of the five thousand. (14:13-20)
• He invited Peter to walk on water. (14:25-29)
• He involved his disciples in the feeding of the four thousand. (15:29-39)

• He took Peter, James, and John with him to witness his transfiguration with Moses and Elijah. (17:1-13)

• He allowed his disciples to try and cast out a demon before he took care of the boy. (17:14-20)

• He involved his disciples in the miracle of the fish providing money for the temple tax. (17:24-27)

Jesus was continually teaching, training, and preparing his disciples for life *after* the resurrection and ascension. As his follower and disciple today, he is inviting you to join him in his work and be a part of all he is doing in the world. Today is all about helping you grow in that partnership with him.

"VERY TRULY I TELL
YOU, WHOEVER
BELIEVES IN ME
WILL DO THE
WORKS I HAVE BEEN
DOING, AND THEY
WILL DO EVEN
GREATER THINGS
THAN THESE,
BECAUSE I AM GOING
TO THE FATHER."

WHAT BIBLE VERSE OR PASSAGE DID YOU MOST CONNECT WITH THIS WEEK? NEXT, WRITE DOWN WHY YOU FEEL THAT MESSAGE CONNECTED AND THE IMPACT IT HAD ON YOU.

WHAT WAS ONE TRUTH OR PRINCIPLE YOU BELIEVE GOD SPOKE TO YOU THIS PAST WEEK?

HAS GOD IMPRESSED ANY NEW THING ON YOU THAT YOU BELIEVE HE WANTS YOU TO BEGIN?

HAS GOD IMPRESSED ANYTHING ON YOU THAT YOU BELIEVE HE WANTS YOU TO SURRENDER—TO SACRIFICE—TO HIM?

THIS WEEK, WAS THERE ANY RELATIONSHIP IN YOUR LIFE
THAT YOU SENSED GOD WANTS YOU TO TAKE ACTION?

A CHRISTIAN FRIEND YOU NEED TO ENCOURAGE?

A NON-CHRISTIAN YOU NEED TO MINISTER TO?

GOD'S WILL

WHAT IS ONE TRUTH YOU LEARNED ABOUT REDEMPTION?

WHAT ONE STEP OF OBEDIENCE DOES GOD WANT
YOU TO TAKE TO CARRY OUT HIS PLAN FOR YOU?

WRITE YOUR PRAYER HERE

Father,

Day 14

PREP & PRAY

I f you are using this Journal in connection with a small group study ... This should be the day of your small group meeting for the *I Still Believe* study. We want to give you the grace and space for two things:

1. If you need to catch up on any day that you may have missed, this time will allow you to be sure you engage fully with *all* the content. If you were pressed for time on any particular day, use this opportunity to go back and review.

2. We want to give you an opportunity to prepare for your group meeting so you can offer all you need to contribute.

Keep in mind:

- YOUR REAL GOAL IS TRANSFORMATION, NOT INFORMATION.
- DON'T JUST ATTEND, BUT EXPERIENCE.
- YOUR PLACE AND CONTRIBUTION IN YOUR GROUP IS VITAL.
- YOUR INTERACTION IS CRUCIAL FOR THE ENTIRE GROUP.
- SOMETHING YOU SAY MIGHT BE THE VERY THING A MEMBER OF YOUR GROUP NEEDS TO HEAR.
- GOD CAN USE YOU TO ENCOURAGE SOMEONE BY YOUR AVAILABILITY AND OBEDIENCE.
- YOU ARE IN YOUR GROUP FOR TWO REASONS: TO GROW AND TO GIVE.

Preparation for Your Small Group Meeting

LOOKING BACK OVER YOUR FIVE DAYS AND CALL TO ACTION,
WRITE DOWN YOUR ANSWERS TO THESE QUESTIONS.

DO YOU HAVE A QUESTION YOU WOULD WANT TO RAISE TO THE GROUP
LEADER FOR FURTHER CLARIFICATION OR DISCUSSION?

WAS THERE ANY CONTENT YOU STRUGGLED TO UNDERSTAND AND
WOULD LIKE TO HAVE CLARITY? (REMEMBER—GETTING YOUR QUESTION
ANSWERED COULD HELP SOMEONE ELSE.)

DID GOD SHOW YOU ANY TRUTH OR PRINCIPLE FROM THE STUDY THIS
WEEK THAT YOU FEEL YOU WOULD LIKE TO SHARE WITH THE GROUP?

CONSIDERING THE SPECIFIC SCRIPTURES FROM THIS WEEK, DID YOU HAVE A
QUESTION OR COMMENT YOU WOULD WANT TO SHARE WITH THE GROUP?

DID SOMETHING SIGNIFICANT HAPPEN IN YOUR WALK WITH GOD THIS
WEEK THAT YOU WOULD LIKE TO SHARE OR REQUEST PRAYER FOR?

HOW WOULD YOU SUM UP YOUR ENGAGEMENT WITH THE *I STILL
BELIEVE* STUDY THIS WEEK IN ONE OR TWO SENTENCES?

Pray for Your Small Group

Take a few minutes to pray for your group meeting. Pray for your leader, each
member by name, and any requests where members have asked for prayer. Ask
God to open your mind and heart to receive what he has for you and also for wisdom in what you need to contribute to your group's dynamic.

If you are using this Journal for your personal study only

Today allows you the opportunity to catch up on the content if needed. The questions below are designed to help you evaluate your experience this week, as well as indicate any area that you may need to seek out help or share with someone. Remember—don't be shy about going to a pastor, church leader, or trusted Christian friend if you realize you have a need.

LOOKING BACK OVER YOUR FIVE DAYS AND CALL TO ACTION,
WRITE DOWN YOUR ANSWERS TO THESE QUESTIONS:

DO YOU HAVE A BIBLICAL OR SPIRITUAL QUESTION
THAT YOU WOULD LIKE TO HAVE ANSWERED?

WAS THERE ANY CONTENT YOU STRUGGLED TO
UNDERSTAND AND WOULD LIKE TO HAVE CLARITY?

DID GOD SHOW YOU ANY TRUTH OR PRINCIPLE FROM THE STUDY THIS WEEK
THAT YOU FEEL YOU NEED TO SHARE WITH SOMEONE IN YOUR LIFE? WHO?

CONSIDERING THE SPECIFIC SCRIPTURES FROM THIS WEEK, DID YOU
HAVE A QUESTION YOU NEED ANSWERED OR SOMETHING YOU FEEL
YOU SHOULD SHARE WITH SOMEONE?

DID SOMETHING SIGNIFICANT HAPPEN IN YOUR WALK WITH GOD THIS
WEEK THAT YOU FEEL YOU NEED TO SHARE WITH SOMEONE AND/OR
ASK THAT PERSON TO PRAY WITH YOU?

HOW WOULD YOU SUM UP YOUR ENGAGEMENT WITH THE
I STILL BELIEVE STUDY THIS WEEK IN ONE OR TWO SENTENCES?

Prayer Time

Take a few minutes to pray for yourself and anyone that God brought to your heart
this week or today in your evaluation. Ask God to open your mind and heart to
receive what he has for you and also for wisdom in any actions you need to take.

Father,

3

YOU ARE
HERE

Grief & Loss

Day 15

THE PEACE OFFERING

I n *I Still Believe*, grief was like an invisible, yet ever-present character in the film. Jeremy's battle with loss was an integral part of the story. Unfortunately, grief will be a part of our own stories in various ways throughout the seasons of our lives. All too often, crises, and tragedies strike unannounced and surprise us with their sudden uninvited company. So in this fallen world, grief and loss are not matters of *if*, but *when*.

THE PEACE OFFERING

Our theme Scripture for this week is a single verse spoken by Jesus to his disciples—John 16:33.

> "I HAVE TOLD YOU THESE THINGS, SO THAT IN ME YOU MAY HAVE PEACE. IN THIS WORLD YOU WILL HAVE TROUBLE. BUT TAKE HEART! I HAVE OVERCOME THE WORLD."

In John 16, Jesus talked to his disciples about two crucial future factors that would profoundly impact all his disciples, including us:

1. Jesus would be leaving to return to the Father, but the Holy Spirit or the "Advocate" would be sent in his place.

2. The disciples would grieve Jesus's loss in the physical sense but experience joy when they realized his Spirit would always be with them.

The culmination of this strange, but miraculous news concluded with today's verse. When Jesus states: "I have told you these things," the two points above are those "things." Let's isolate the next three phrases to take a deeper look.

"... SO THAT IN ME YOU MAY HAVE PEACE."

Jesus provided the opportunity for all sinners to have peace with a holy God. The opportunity is not a mandate, but a choice. He has made his peace available, but he will not or does not force it upon us. We choose whether or not to accept and receive his peace. This dynamic is exactly why we can come to terms with a situation and be at peace, but then something dramatically changes and we "lose our peace." Of course, we don't actually lose it. We change our focus to the circumstances from the peace he offers.

Yet where Christ is present, peace is always available.

"IN THIS WORLD YOU WILL HAVE TROUBLE."

Because God is sovereign, omniscient, and almighty, upon salvation he could choose to remove all our troubles for the rest of our days. But he doesn't. Troubles continue. Troubles will come. In fact, ironically, sometimes following Jesus creates more problems for us as we are obedient to him and do not follow the world. But the trouble remains so we may experience him in a much greater, deeper, and stronger capacity.

Troubles will come and go, but Jesus's peace is always there.

"BUT TAKE HEART! I HAVE OVERCOME THE WORLD."

Paul offered the best explanation of this concept in Romans 8:35 and 37:

> WHO SHALL SEPARATE US FROM THE LOVE OF CHRIST? SHALL
> TROUBLE OR HARDSHIP OR PERSECUTION OR FAMINE OR
> NAKEDNESS OR DANGER OR SWORD? … NO, IN ALL THESE
> THINGS WE ARE MORE THAN CONQUERORS THROUGH HIM
> WHO LOVED US.

We can overcome because Jesus has overcome.

THE BIG PICTURE PERSPECTIVE

The story is told of two artists who were commissioned to provide oil paintings depicting an artistic interpretation of peace. On the day of the unveiling, one artist had created a beautiful landscape with lush, rolling green hills, massive oak trees, with the centerpiece being a tranquil stream meandering through the valley. But as the cover was removed from the second painting, a very different scene emerged. The canvas held the image of a violent waterfall crashing onto jagged rocks with a dark mist masking the backdrop. Upon a closer look, besides the cascading torrent was a small, fragile tree clinging to the mountainside. A tiny nest was nestled into the branches. Inside the nest, sat a mother sparrow, perfectly dry and fast asleep.

When Jesus was born, the priest Zechariah said, "Praise be to the Lord, the God of Israel, because he has come to his people and redeemed them" (Luke 1:68). While we all want to live in the first picture every day, our reality is that of the second picture, particularly when we rest in the peace Christ provides us in the chaos. While the world is crashing noisily around us, we may experience peace.

If you surveyed people regarding the definition and connotation of peace in our culture, you would likely hear more about the absence of trouble than the presence of contentment. To experience the promise of John 16:33, we are not seeking to subtract anything from life, but rather simply add Jesus to every circumstance.

Take a look at The Message Bible's version on John 16:33:

> "I'VE TOLD YOU ALL THIS SO THAT TRUSTING ME, YOU WILL BE UNSHAKABLE AND ASSURED, DEEPLY AT PEACE. IN THIS GODLESS WORLD YOU WILL CONTINUE TO EXPERIENCE DIFFICULTIES. BUT TAKE

> "I love John 16:33. Jesus is actually telling his disciples, 'You're going to face trials.' We don't want to hear that part of the promise. But his comfort at the end of that verse says, 'No matter what you experience, I've overcome that. I went through pain. I went through grief. I overcame. And now you can overcome those things through me because I've experienced them.' Jesus empowers us to walk through the pain and give us whatever we need to battle those things."

JEREMY CAMP

getting personal

JESUS TOLD HIS DISCIPLES THAT HE WOULD BE LEAVING SOON, BUT HIS SPIRIT WOULD BE STAYING WITH THEM AND THAT THEIR GRIEF WOULD TURN TO JOY. HOW WOULD YOU HAVE FELT HEARING HIS WORDS?

WHAT ARE SOME OF THE MAJOR DIFFERENCES BETWEEN THE CIRCUMSTANTIAL PEACE OF THE WORLD AND THE BIBLICAL PEACE JESUS OFFERS?

BY HIS MAKING PEACE A CHOICE AS AN OPPORTUNITY TO YOU, WHAT DO YOU THINK GOD ULTIMATELY WANTS FOR YOUR LIFE?

WRITE YOUR THOUGHTS ABOUT THIS STATEMENT: "TROUBLES WILL COME AND GO, BUT JESUS'S PEACE IS ALWAYS THERE." WHY DO WE SO OFTEN SEE TROUBLE AS MORE OF A CONSTANT THAN PEACE?

WHY DO MOST PEOPLE VIEW PEACE AS THE ABSENCE OF TROUBLE RATHER THAN THE PRESENCE OF CONTENTMENT?

JEREMY STATED: "JESUS EMPOWERS US TO WALK THROUGH THE PAIN AND GIVE US WHATEVER WE NEED TO BATTLE THOSE THINGS." HOW DOES THIS TRUTH ENCOURAGE YOU TODAY?

FILL IN THE BLANKS TO CREATE A CLOSING PRAYER:

LORD JESUS, HERE ARE MY TROUBLES CREATING GRIEF IN MY LIFE TODAY:

3

Day 16

MATTERS OF LIFE AND DEATH

"People have often asked me, 'Do you think you have healed from everything that happened with Melissa?' I look at it like when you get a cut, a big open wound. For a while, it's this wound that you have to heal. It takes a while. Sometimes you have to get stitches. But soon it does heal up and you don't have that pain, that constant nagging there. Yet you can still see the scar. With grief, you're going to have a scar. There's going to be some lasting effects in your life, things that you have to deal with. For example, I've battled with trust for a long time. That's something I've struggled with because, like you see in the film, I really believed that God was going to heal Melissa. I felt like he gave me a promise. And when that didn't happen, I was disappointed with God and at first said, 'I don't know if I can trust you.' I had those feelings for a while."

JEREMY CAMP

MATTERS OF LIFE AND DEATH

One of the principles we can take away from Jeremy's story is that God is okay with us expressing our honest feelings with him. He already knows what and how we feel, so better to get out our emotions with him than let them stay inside and potentially poison our hearts. And, of course, our ultimate example is Jesus. He was always direct and transparent whether talking to his Father or the people around him. Today, let's look at one of the most intriguing accounts in the Gospels recorded in John 11.

Sisters Mary and Martha were two of Jesus's closest friends. They had a brother named Lazarus, who was also close to Jesus. Lazarus became very ill so they sent word to Jesus so he could come and heal Lazarus. When he finally arrived, Lazarus had already been dead and entombed for four days.

When they saw Jesus coming, Martha went out to meet him and very honestly, but politely stated, "If you had gotten here sooner, my brother would still be alive." Yet knowing whom she was addressing, Martha added, "But I know that not even death can stop God from giving you whatever you ask." Being forthright was quickly followed up by her faith. Mary and a group of mourners then came to join Jesus and Martha.

WHEN JESUS SAW HER WEEPING, AND THE JEWS WHO HAD COME ALONG WITH HER ALSO WEEPING, HE WAS DEEPLY MOVED IN SPIRIT AND TROUBLED. "WHERE HAVE YOU LAID HIM?" HE ASKED. "COME AND SEE, LORD," THEY REPLIED. JESUS WEPT. THEN THE JEWS SAID, "SEE HOW HE LOVED HIM!" ... JESUS, ONCE MORE DEEPLY MOVED, CAME TO THE TOMB. IT WAS A CAVE WITH A STONE LAID ACROSS THE ENTRANCE. "TAKE AWAY THE STONE," HE SAID. ... SO THEY TOOK AWAY THE STONE. THEN JESUS LOOKED UP AND SAID, "FATHER, I THANK YOU THAT YOU HAVE HEARD ME. I KNEW THAT YOU ALWAYS HEAR ME, BUT I SAID THIS FOR THE BENEFIT OF THE PEOPLE STANDING HERE, THAT THEY MAY BELIEVE THAT YOU SENT ME." WHEN HE HAD SAID THIS, JESUS CALLED IN A LOUD VOICE, "LAZARUS, COME OUT!" THE DEAD MAN CAME OUT, HIS HANDS AND FEET WRAPPED WITH STRIPS OF LINEN, AND A CLOTH AROUND HIS FACE. JESUS SAID TO THEM, "TAKE OFF THE GRAVE

CLOTHES AND LET HIM GO."
THEREFORE MANY OF THE
JEWS WHO HAD COME TO
VISIT MARY, AND HAD SEEN
WHAT JESUS DID, BELIEVED
IN HIM.

—JOHN 11:33-36, 38, 41-45

THE MINISTRY OF TEARS

The most fascinating aspect of Lazarus's story is that Jesus knew he was about to raise Lazarus from the dead, so his own emotion was simply triggered by witnessing and feeling the deep hurt of his friends. Jesus showed us that feeling emotion and connecting with others in their pain is a way of ministering in silence. His tears were just as powerful as his words that were about to free Lazarus and change the circumstances.

Albert Schweitzer was in Africa involved in medical missionary work during World War II. One day at N'Gomo, he was standing on the bank of the Lambarene River watching a steamer boat vanish into the distance, leaving its big, black trail of smoke in the sky.

His attention was suddenly drawn to a woman sitting on the bank, weeping. He realized her son had been taken by force by a group of young men from the village to fight in the war, as was a common practice of the army. Her kidnapped son was on that boat. She was wracked with grief, knowing she might never see him again.

As a physician, did he offer her some remedy for what would become sleepless nights? As a philosopher, did he recite a monologue of wisdom from one of the greats to change her mind? As a theologian, did he sit down and quote Scripture as a reminder to her of God's power?

No, none of these. He responded as a fellow human being. Schweitzer wrote, "I took hold of her hand and wanted to comfort her, but she went on crying as if she did not hear me. Suddenly I felt that I was crying with her, silently, towards the setting sun, as she was."

True compassion is a gift from God and a deep ministry to people. Drawing back to Jeremy's testimony, this response always requires a total honesty of heart toward God, ourselves, and those we encounter.

TRUE *compassion*
IS A GIFT FROM GOD
AND A DEEP MINISTRY
TO PEOPLE.

getting personal

REGARDING JEREMY'S ANALOGY OF GRIEF AS A WOUND THAT MUST HEAL BUT THEN BECOMES A SCAR THAT CAN HAVE LINGERING OR LASTING EFFECTS, WHAT ARE YOUR THOUGHTS?

CONSIDERING JEREMY'S HONEST CONFESSION OF DEALING WITH DISAPPOINTMENT BECAUSE GOD DIDN'T DO WHAT HE THOUGHT HE WOULD DO, WHY IS IT OFTEN DIFFICULT FOR US TO BE HONEST ABOUT THOSE KINDS OF FEELINGS AS CHRISTIANS?

WHAT EMOTIONS DO YOU THINK MARY AND MARTHA DEALT WITH FOLLOWING THEIR BROTHER'S DEATH AND DURING JESUS'S APPARENT DELAY?

WHY DO YOU SUPPOSE JESUS JOINED THE SISTERS IN THEIR EMOTIONS RATHER THAN JUST TELLING THEM TO STOP CRYING AND EXPLAIN WANT HE WAS ABOUT TO DO?

WHAT CAN WE TAKE AWAY FROM JESUS AND SCHWEITZER'S RESPONSE TO WITNESSING AND MINISTERING TO OTHERS' PAIN?

MOST OF US WOULD LIKELY AGREE THAT THE WORLD IS BECOMING MORE CALLOUSED TO TRAGEDY AND TRUE COMPASSION SEEMS TO BE A DYING ART. AS A CHRIST-FOLLOWER, HOW CAN YOU TRY AND AVOID ADAPTING TO THE CULTURE BUT STAY CONNECTED TO THE HEART OF JESUS TO KNOW WHEN TO WAIT, WHEN TO CRY WITH SOMEONE, AND WHEN TO TAKE ACTION?

Day 17

THE JUDAS FACTOR

One of the greatest losses we can experience is the death of a relationship. In fact, there are times a separation or an ending to a marriage, family connection, or friendship can feel worse than death. Death offers a final resolution that we can do nothing about, but when someone just stops being a part of our lives, that absence can be devastating and one of the worst losses we can experience.

As a human on the earth for thirty-three years, Jesus experienced everything we deal with, including the betrayal of a friend in his closest circle. Judas was not an enemy from the outside or some fringe follower that went off the rails. He was one of his chosen twelve. Judas had witnessed the miracles. He had sat around the campfire at night and heard Jesus talk of God and Heaven on a very intimate level. Yet he turned on his friend and his God.

NOW THE PASSOVER AND THE FESTIVAL OF UNLEAVENED BREAD WERE ONLY TWO DAYS AWAY, AND THE CHIEF PRIESTS AND THE TEACHERS OF THE LAW WERE SCHEMING TO ARREST JESUS SECRETLY AND KILL HIM.

—MARK 14:1

After the disciples had witnessed the woman anoint Jesus's feet with expensive perfume and questioned the act as a waste of money, he rebuked them, essentially saying she was worshipping and foreshadowing his burial anointing that was soon to come. Whether this circumstance triggered Judas's response or not, he had his change of heart that night and decided to sell Jesus out.

THEN JUDAS ISCARIOT, ONE OF THE TWELVE, WENT TO THE CHIEF PRIESTS TO BETRAY JESUS TO THEM. THEY WERE DELIGHTED TO HEAR THIS AND PROMISED TO GIVE HIM MONEY. SO HE WATCHED FOR AN OPPORTUNITY TO HAND HIM OVER.

—MARK 14:10-11

At the event that we now use to regularly commemorate and remember Jesus's sacrifice—the Last Supper—he spoke of the betrayal and also Peter's denial. Then everyone but Judas went to Gethsemane.

JUST AS HE WAS SPEAKING, JUDAS, ONE OF THE TWELVE, APPEARED. WITH HIM WAS A CROWD ARMED WITH SWORDS AND CLUBS, SENT FROM THE CHIEF PRIESTS, THE TEACHERS OF THE LAW, AND THE ELDERS. NOW THE BETRAYER HAD ARRANGED A SIGNAL WITH THEM: "THE ONE I KISS IS THE MAN; ARREST HIM AND LEAD HIM AWAY UNDER GUARD." GOING AT ONCE TO JESUS, JUDAS SAID, "RABBI!" AND KISSED HIM. THE MEN SEIZED JESUS AND ARRESTED HIM.

—MARK 14:43-46

As a part of the Trinity and being one hundred percent God, Jesus knew from day one that Judas would be the linchpin for his crucifixion. Peter only added insult to injury. Yet he called and befriended them anyway. God's unconditional love and grace are on display in those relationships as much as any in history.

In the late 1960s, Chiu-Chin-Hsiu and Ho-Hsiu-Tzu were two Christian girls that had been sentenced to execution by the Chinese government for refusing to deny Christ. As they stood in the prison yard surrounded by armed guards, the executioner began to walk toward them with a pistol in his hand. When he stepped up to them, they realized he was their pastor, who had also been sentenced to die with the girls.

But as has often happened throughout the history of martyrdom, the persecutors managed to turn him against them for the promise of freedom. He would be set free if he shot the girls who had once been under his ministry. The soldiers promised to release him if he would execute the girls. He accepted.

Exhibiting a deep faith, the girls respectfully bowed before their pastor. One of them said, "Before you shoot us, we wish to thank you heartily for what you have meant to us. You taught us that Christians are sometimes weak and commit terrible sins, but they can be forgiven again. When you regret what you are about to do to us, do not despair like Judas, but repent like Peter. God bless you, and remember that our last thought was not one of indignation against your failure. Everyone passes through hours of darkness. May God reward you for all the good you have done to us. We die with gratitude."

The pastor pulled the trigger twice and then the guards shot him.

This documented testimony of martyrdom proves the miraculous peace of Christ is available even in the most extreme circumstances of betrayal and threat.

Like death, grief, and loss, betrayal in relationships will come into our lives. So the real decision we must make is how we will respond. The world tells us how to handle betrayal. Social media shouts what to do with betrayers. But Christ has shown us what to do. The two Chinese martyred teenagers followed his example of forgiveness and freedom to the end to become incredible inspirational testimonies to others in the Underground Church.

King David understood betrayal from both sides. He had been betrayed by his predecessor, Saul, and his own son, Absalom. But David had learned how to handle betrayal by being the betrayer to God and his brothers-in-arms through his adultery, lies, and murder of Uriah. Psalm 51 is one of the most beautiful chapters of the Bible because the text shows us how to approach God when we become the betrayer.

> HAVE MERCY ON ME, O GOD, ACCORDING TO YOUR UNFAILING LOVE; ACCORDING TO YOUR GREAT COMPASSION BLOT OUT MY TRANSGRESSIONS. … MY SACRIFICE, O GOD, IS A BROKEN SPIRIT; A BROKEN AND CONTRITE HEART YOU, GOD, WILL NOT DESPISE.
>
> —PSALM 51:1, 17

In Psalm 89, God is talking about David and his sons when he promises:

> "BUT I WILL NOT TAKE MY LOVE FROM HIM, NOR WILL I EVER BETRAY MY FAITHFULNESS. I WILL NOT VIOLATE MY COVENANT OR ALTER WHAT MY LIPS HAVE UTTERED"
>
> —PSALM 89:33-34

God tells us though we may be betrayed and become the betrayer, he will never betray his faithfulness to us. What an encouraging and incredible promise for us to remember when we experience pain in relationships. This promise can lead us out of bitterness and hatred and into forgiveness and freedom in the spirit of Psalm 51.

> **"For us, it's just deepened our walks with the Lord. It's the new normal. All of a sudden things that you have to battle that maybe you never battled before like trust or fear, you learn again to know that God is trustworthy and he's faithful, even amidst the craziest things, the fear of that pain again, but God is in the midst of that."**
>
> ADRIENNE CAMP

WHY IS BETRAYAL ONE OF THE MOST PAINFUL EXPERIENCES WE CAN
EXPERIENCE IN LIFE?

WHAT MAKES DEATH SOMETIMES EASIER TO DEAL WITH THAN
BETRAYAL?

HOW DO YOU THINK JESUS'S ETERNAL PERSPECTIVE MAY HAVE HELPED
HIM WHEN HE KNEW THROUGHOUT HIS ENTIRE MINISTRY THAT JUDAS
WOULD BETRAY HIM, AND PETER WOULD DENY HIM?

WE KNOW THAT JUDAS'S LIFE ENDED TRAGICALLY WHILE PETER WENT ON TO BECOME A FOUNDATIONAL PART OF THE EARLY CHURCH. WHAT DO YOU THINK MADE THE DIFFERENCE IN THE TWO MEN'S CHOICES AND THEIR RESPONSE TO WHAT THEY DID TO JESUS?

WHILE THE STORY OF THE TWO CHINESE MARTYRS IS VERY DIFFICULT TO READ, HOW DOES A TESTIMONY LIKE THIS INSPIRE YOU IN FORGIVENESS AND PERSONAL FREEDOM?

TAKE A MOMENT TO READ PSALM 51 AND THEN WRITE OUT YOUR THOUGHTS TO COMPLETE THIS SENTENCE. GOD, I KNOW YOU ARE FAITHFUL TO ME BECAUSE:

Day 18

GOD'S GRIEF, GOD'S MAN

Jeremy Camp's dad has clearly been a stabilizing and steadfast force of support and strength in his life. Their deep relationship is clear in the film. There is a scene in *I Still Believe* where Jeremy is asking his dad how he has survived walking through so many difficult seasons. Jeremy shares:

> **"My dad says, 'My life isn't full in spite of all these things that have happened to me, but because of them. They are why I have a full life.' It's because of the perspective you gain and the character and the things that you learn in the midst of the pain. Your life is full because of these things you've learned because you have gotten to see God come through and then you know he's faithful."**
>
> **JEREMY CAMP**

So living the abundant life in Christ is not about a lack of bad things happening, but rather the strength and character built in our endurance from walking through those events.

GOD'S GRIEF, GOD'S MAN

One of the worst accounts of loss and the saddest stories of grief in the Bible is found early on in Genesis 6. This experience is not about any man but God himself.

> THE LORD SAW
> HOW GREAT THE
> WICKEDNESS OF
> THE HUMAN RACE
> HAD BECOME ON
> THE EARTH, AND

THAT EVERY INCLINATION OF THE THOUGHTS
OF THE HUMAN HEART WAS ONLY EVIL ALL
THE TIME. THE LORD REGRETTED THAT HE
HAD MADE HUMAN BEINGS ON THE EARTH,
AND HIS HEART WAS DEEPLY TROUBLED. SO
THE LORD SAID, "I WILL WIPE FROM THE FACE
OF THE EARTH THE HUMAN RACE I HAVE
CREATED—AND WITH THEM THE ANIMALS, THE
BIRDS AND THE CREATURES THAT MOVE ALONG
THE GROUND—FOR I REGRET THAT I HAVE
MADE THEM." BUT NOAH FOUND FAVOR IN THE
EYES OF THE LORD.

—GENESIS 6:5-8

Through much of the later books of the Prophets, we see God's anger manifested because of issues such as idol worship. Verse 5 paints a picture of a deeper problem—the sheer presence of pure evil. The language used here indicates their very motives were driven by, what? "Only evil." How often? "All the time." That leaves no room for goodness, kindness, or righteousness of any kind. The fruit eaten by Adam and Eve had thoroughly poisoned the next generations.

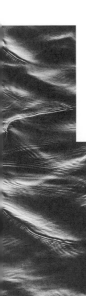

As a holy God, the only way to get rid of the evil was to destroy his creation.

Verse 6 states that God was regretful, grieved, and "deeply troubled" by what he witnessed. This does not translate as anger but rather a deep hurt. In short, God was heartbroken by how far his creation had moved away from his heart.

As a holy God, the only way to get rid of the evil was to destroy his creation. The one who makes has the right to destroy. The builder has the ability to tear down and start over. Verse 7 is one of the only times in Scripture we see God express regret. He knows there is an ever-growing mess that now must be cleaned up. But the very fact that humans were given the freedom to make the mess is because God is love and chose to give free choice, even to the extreme of his creation fully betraying him and his ways.

But then God saw one man and his family and that changed everything. Noah chose to be the exception to the rule. Noah decided to follow God no matter who else did. He was righteous—loved God—and blameless among the people—loved his neighbor. Noah didn't know about Jesus. The Holy Spirit had not yet come. He had never heard the Gospel. Noah was simply obedient to God because it was the right and best thing to do.

GOD'S GOODNESS, GOD'S PLAN

So God would use Noah to rebuild and repopulate the earth. He found favor in the eyes of God. Following the flood and the journey of the ark, we see the redemption and promise he made even though humans would once again choose the enemy over him and evil over good.

THEN NOAH BUILT AN ALTAR TO THE LORD AND, TAKING
SOME OF ALL THE CLEAN ANIMALS AND CLEAN BIRDS, HE
SACRIFICED BURNT OFFERINGS ON IT. THE LORD SMELLED
THE PLEASING AROMA AND SAID IN HIS HEART: "NEVER AGAIN
WILL I CURSE THE GROUND BECAUSE OF HUMANS, EVEN
THOUGH EVERY INCLINATION OF THE HUMAN HEART IS EVIL
FROM CHILDHOOD. AND NEVER AGAIN WILL I DESTROY ALL
LIVING CREATURES, AS I HAVE DONE.

- GENESIS 8:20-21

When Noah and his family came out of the ark onto the land, he designated some animals for an offering to God. Biblical scholars tell us this was not a sin offering or thank offering, but rather one to ask for God's blessing as they began their new lives.

God responded by promising to never destroy his creation again and in verses 15 to 18 even repeated some of his original blessing and command given to Adam and Eve—stewardship of creation and freedom to populate the planet.

In that moment, God knew there would be only one more sacrifice to deal with sin once and for all—his only Son. The problem of sin separating mankind from God would be taken care of by the cross. He would pay the debt of disobedience, providing a bridge to a relationship with the Father.

In Matthew 24 and Luke 17, Jesus uses the time of Noah as the example for how it will be on the day of his Second Coming. Just like the day the rain began, people going about their busy lives, not thinking at all about the Kingdom of God, so it will be on the day he returns. But the skies will not be filled with rain, but the glory of Christ coming for his people.

May the story of Noah remind us that, while the days in which we live are also evil, we have the freedom to follow God. His ways will always provide the best path in life. ■

HE WILL ALWAYS

PROVIDE THE BEST

path in life.

getting personal

WHAT ARE YOUR THOUGHTS ABOUT JEREMY'S DAD'S COMMENT: "MY LIFE ISN'T FULL IN SPITE OF ALL THESE THINGS THAT HAVE HAPPENED TO ME, BUT BECAUSE OF THEM"?

UNDERSTANDING GOD'S BROKEN HEART IN THE STORY OF NOAH, HOW DOES THIS CHALLENGE YOU IN YOUR OWN CHOICES OF OBEDIENCE?

DO YOU SEE ANY CONNECTIONS BETWEEN THE STORY OF NOAH AND THE ARK AND JESUS AND THE CROSS? EXPLAIN.

WAS THERE ANYTHING IN THE STORY OF NOAH THAT YOU HAD NOT
NOTICED BEFORE? EXPLAIN.

WHAT IS ONE TAKEAWAY FROM THE NOAH STORY YOU CAN APPLY IN
YOUR OWN EXPERIENCES OF LOSS AND GRIEF?

COMPLETE THE OPEN-ENDED SENTENCE:

FATHER, I KNOW I HAVE FOUND FAVOR IN YOUR EYES BECAUSE:

Day 19

BEAUTY FROM ASHES

S tudying the tough issues of life and faith such as grief and loss can be difficult. Yet, addressing our painful experiences to see what God might have to say to us as well as choosing to deal with our hurts is vital to our health and growth. Today, we will close out the content portion of this topic on an encouraging note—how God can bring beauty from ashes.

WHO MOURN, AND PROVIDE FOR THOSE WHO GRIEVE IN ZION—TO BESTOW ON THEM A CROWN OF

THE SPIRIT OF THE SOVEREIGN LORD IS ON ME, BECAUSE THE LORD HAS ANOINTED ME TO PROCLAIM GOOD NEWS TO THE POOR. HE HAS SENT ME TO BIND UP THE BROKENHEARTED, TO PROCLAIM FREEDOM FOR THE CAPTIVES AND RELEASE FROM DARKNESS FOR THE PRISONERS, TO PROCLAIM THE YEAR OF THE LORD'S FAVOR AND THE DAY OF VENGEANCE OF OUR GOD, TO COMFORT ALL

BEAUTY INSTEAD OF ASHES, THE OIL OF JOY INSTEAD OF MOURNING, AND A GARMENT OF PRAISE INSTEAD OF A SPIRIT OF DESPAIR. THEY WILL BE CALLED OAKS OF RIGHTEOUSNESS, A PLANTING OF THE LORD FOR THE DISPLAY OF HIS SPLENDOR.

- ISAIAH 61:1-3

> **"After trials and grief, there's gratitude for beautiful things, for relationships, for the things that are not distracting. We get so busy and caught up in so many things that really are meaningless. But when you go through trials it's like the things that need to be shaken, get shaken, and the things that are important, remain. A quote by Elizabeth Elliot is: 'God will not protect you from anything that will make you more like Christ.' When the shaking happens and all those unnecessary things fall away, God uses that to purify us and make us more like Jesus."**

ADRIENNE CAMP

The words of Isaiah in today's passage are not only for us to experience personally, but also for us to choose to become the messengers and ministers who deliver these miraculous gifts to others in Jesus' name. The burdens and pain of our grief and loss can become connecting points to share God's love, grace, mercy, and healing to those he allows us to influence and impact.

Considering yesterday's story of Noah, have you ever considered how seemingly strange it sounds for God to place the responsibility and opportunity of sharing the plan of salvation for the human race back into the very hands of those that created the problem to begin with? But that is exactly what he has done!

BEAUTIFUL SCARS

On our second day this week, Jeremy used the analogy of emotional scars from our personal hurts being like physical scars that no one can see. Expanding on those thoughts, God can use those scars to be the connecting points for us to make the Gospel real and relevant to those around us. The issues in our lives that bring the need for salvation also become the conversation pieces to draw others to him.

The scars on our hearts can be cuts created by a(n):

Abusive parent or caregiver
Jealous sibling
Bitter teacher or coach
Insecure friend
Toxic family member
Cyber bully

Regardless of where they came from, you know your scars and their source well. You know who cut you, the circumstances, and possibly down to the details of the day and time. Maybe for you, someone continued the pattern of abuse over years. Whether you have a few nicks or severe lacerations, scars can infect us, define us, limit our relationships, and even create a distrust of God.

When you see an old physical scar, you can know the cut has healed, but there's a deformity of some kind left on the skin. The problem with scars of the heart is you see them only in and through a person's behavior. A physical scar may look bad, but no longer causes pain. A scar on the heart is invisible to the eye but can cause deep hurts every day.

Jesus Christ understands our scars. As God, he could have avoided them altogether. But he didn't. He also understands what it takes to heal even the most painful of scars.

Just before today's passage in Isaiah, he wrote in chapter 53 some surprising prophetic words about Jesus:

> HE HAD NO BEAUTY OR MAJESTY TO ATTRACT US TO HIM, NOTHING IN HIS APPEARANCE THAT WE SHOULD DESIRE HIM. HE WAS DESPISED AND REJECTED BY MANKIND, A MAN OF SUFFERING, AND FAMILIAR WITH PAIN. LIKE ONE FROM WHOM PEOPLE HIDE THEIR FACES HE WAS DESPISED, AND WE HELD HIM IN LOW ESTEEM
>
> - ISAIAH 53:2-3

Interestingly, this passage calls into question many of the historic artistic depictions of Jesus as a strikingly handsome man. Isaiah moves on to describe the experience of the crucifixion:

> SURELY HE TOOK UP OUR PAIN AND BORE OUR SUFFERING, YET WE CONSIDERED HIM PUNISHED BY GOD, STRICKEN BY HIM, AND AFFLICTED. BUT HE WAS PIERCED FOR OUR TRANSGRESSIONS, HE WAS CRUSHED FOR OUR INIQUITIES; THE PUNISHMENT THAT BROUGHT US PEACE WAS ON HIM, AND BY HIS WOUNDS WE ARE HEALED. WE ALL, LIKE SHEEP, HAVE GONE ASTRAY, EACH OF US HAS TURNED TO OUR OWN WAY; AND THE LORD HAS LAID ON HIM THE INIQUITY OF US ALL.
>
> - ISAIAH 53:4-6

THE LORD HAS LAID ON HIM
THE INIQUITY OF US ALL.

ISAIAH 53:6

The reality of these powerful verses is that it was our pain he carried—our disfigurements—all the things wrong with us. He did not bring these things on himself, but it was our sin that ripped and tore and crushed him. He took our punishment. His act of the greatest love the world will ever see made us whole. Through his scars we can be healed.

This life is going to create scars—external and internal. It's what we do with our cuts, wounds, and scars that make the difference. It's how we respond to pain that can change our lives; allowing God to do what only he can do—heal us. He won't make us forget painful memories, but he can heal us from feeling the pain every day. And then use those scars as beautiful testimonies to invite others to the Healer. ∎

getting personal

LOOKING AGAIN AT ISAIAH 61:1-3, WRITE DOWN THE MINISTRIES LISTED IN WHICH GOD CAN USE US AS HIS FOLLOWERS IN OTHER'S LIVES. FOR EXAMPLE, THE FIRST IS "PROCLAIM GOOD NEWS TO THE POOR."

LOOKING AGAIN AT ADRIENNE'S QUOTE, HAS THERE BEEN A TIME IN YOUR LIFE WHERE YOU HAVE BEEN SHAKEN AND THE OUTCOME CAUSED YOU TO PUT LIFE IN PERSPECTIVE AND RE-PRIORITIZE? EXPLAIN.

IN THE DISCUSSION OF OUR SCARS AND THEIR SOURCE IN OUR LIVES, WHAT CAME TO MIND FOR YOU?

IN READING THE TWO ISAIAH 53 PASSAGES, WHAT STRUCK YOU THE MOST IN THE PROPHET'S WORDS ABOUT JESUS. BE SPECIFIC.

IN CLOSING TODAY, IS THERE A SOURCE OF GRIEF, A CAUSE OF PAIN, OR A SCAR THIS WEEK'S CONTENT HAS REVEALED THAT YOU KNOW YOU NEED TO SURRENDER TO THE LORD FOR HIS HEALING? MAYBE YOU REALIZE YOU NEED SOME OUTSIDE HELP? MAYBE YOU NEED TO FORGIVE SOMEONE OR ASK FOR FORGIVENESS? WRITE DOWN YOUR THOUGHTS AND FEELINGS HERE.

LASTLY, WRITE OUT A PRAYER FOR WHAT YOU NEED GOD TO DO WITH YOUR PAIN AND YOUR SCARS, AND THEN READ IT OUT LOUD TO HIM.

Day 20

CALL TO ACTION

Since this is your third week, you know that today is all about getting a plan for application and living out what you have been shown through the content. Following through with this sixth day is crucial to help you carry the truths you learn past these five weeks to become a part of your spiritual foundation in Christ.

In all the belief systems that ever existed before, those that exist now, and will ever exist, there is one pattern that all have in common: As a non-believer of any belief system, you are ignorant of the necessary knowledge needed to be enlightened. So you must hear and receive the information, which you either reject or receive.

Reception of the information can become revelation—the full acceptance of the belief system as personal truth. Reception ends the ignorance. Revelation begins the belief. Most belief systems end here. Once you have received and accepted the information and are enlightened, you are considered to be a follower of that belief.

To recap:

• FOR ANY BELIEF SYSTEM, YOU CHOOSE REJECTION OR RECEPTION.

• RECEPTION CAN BRING REVELATION.

• REVELATION BRINGS BELIEF.

• BELIEF CAN BRING A GREATER LEVEL OF RECEPTION. AND THE CYCLE CONTINUES.

But Jesus came along and added *another* step, a *new* step to belief. He taught that obedience of the belief—the action following the knowledge—is what makes the difference in those who follow him. You see the knowledge carried out into action. That is what this day is all about. To get to the last step in what Jesus taught us—obedience and application of what you learn.

WHAT BIBLE VERSE OR PASSAGE DID YOU MOST CONNECT WITH THIS
WEEK? NEXT, WRITE DOWN WHY YOU FEEL THAT MESSAGE CONNECTED
AND THE IMPACT IT HAD ON YOU.

WHAT WAS ONE TRUTH OR PRINCIPLE YOU
BELIEVE GOD SPOKE TO YOU THIS PAST WEEK?

HAS GOD IMPRESSED ANY NEW THING ON YOU
THAT YOU BELIEVE HE WANTS YOU TO BEGIN?

HAS GOD IMPRESSED ANYTHING ON YOU THAT YOU
BELIEVE HE WANTS YOU TO SURRENDER TO HIM?

THIS WEEK, WAS THERE ANY RELATIONSHIP IN YOUR LIFE
THAT YOU SENSED GOD WANTS YOU TO TAKE ACTION?

A CHRISTIAN FRIEND YOU NEED TO ENCOURAGE?

A NON-CHRISTIAN YOU NEED TO MINISTER TO?

GOD'S WILL

WHAT IS ONE TRUTH YOU LEARNED ABOUT
DEALING WITH GRIEF AND LOSS?

WHAT ONE STEP OF OBEDIENCE DOES GOD WANT
YOU TO TAKE TO CARRY OUT HIS PLAN FOR YOU?

Day 21

PREP & PRAY

I f you are using this Journal in connection with a small group study ... This should be the day of your small group meeting for the *I Still Believe* study. We want to give you the grace and space for two things:

1. If you need to catch up on any day that you may have missed, this time will allow you to be sure you engage fully with *all* the content. If you were pressed for time on any particular day, use this opportunity to go back and review.

2. We want to give you an opportunity to prepare for your group meeting so you can offer all you need to contribute.

Keep in mind:

• YOUR REAL GOAL IS TRANSFORMATION, NOT INFORMATION.

• DON'T JUST ATTEND, BUT EXPERIENCE.

• YOUR PLACE AND CONTRIBUTION IN YOUR GROUP IS VITAL.

• YOUR INTERACTION IS CRUCIAL FOR THE ENTIRE GROUP.

• SOMETHING YOU SAY MIGHT BE THE VERY THING A MEMBER OF YOUR GROUP NEEDS TO HEAR.

• GOD CAN USE YOU TO ENCOURAGE SOMEONE BY YOUR AVAIL ABILITY AND OBEDIENCE.

• YOU ARE IN YOUR GROUP FOR TWO REASONS: TO GROW AND TO GIVE.

Preparation for Your Small Group Meeting

LOOKING BACK OVER YOUR FIVE DAYS AND CALL TO ACTION, WRITE
DOWN YOUR ANSWERS TO THESE QUESTIONS. IF ANY OF THESE
DON'T APPLY TO YOUR WEEK, SKIP TO THE NEXT QUESTION:

DO YOU HAVE A QUESTION YOU WOULD WANT TO RAISE TO THE GROUP
LEADER FOR FURTHER CLARIFICATION OR DISCUSSION?

WAS THERE ANY CONTENT YOU STRUGGLED TO UNDERSTAND AND
WOULD LIKE TO HAVE CLARITY? (REMEMBER—GETTING YOUR QUESTION
ANSWERED COULD HELP SOMEONE ELSE.)

DID GOD SHOW YOU ANY TRUTH OR PRINCIPLE FROM THE STUDY THIS
WEEK THAT YOU FEEL YOU WOULD LIKE TO SHARE WITH THE GROUP?

CONSIDERING THE SPECIFIC SCRIPTURES FROM THIS WEEK, DID YOU HAVE A
QUESTION OR COMMENT YOU WOULD WANT TO SHARE WITH THE GROUP?

DID SOMETHING SIGNIFICANT HAPPEN IN YOUR WALK WITH GOD THIS WEEK THAT YOU WOULD LIKE TO SHARE OR REQUEST PRAYER FOR?

HOW WOULD YOU SUM UP YOUR ENGAGEMENT WITH THE *I STILL BELIEVE* STUDY THIS WEEK IN ONE OR TWO SENTENCES?

Pray for Your Small Group

Take a few minutes to pray for your group meeting. Pray for:

- Your leader
- Each member
- Any ongoing requests of your members
- God to open your mind and heart to receive what he has for you
- Wisdom in what you need to contribute to your group's dynamic

If you are using this Journal for your personal study only

Today allows you the opportunity to catch up on the content if needed. The questions below are designed to help you evaluate your experience this week, as well as indicate any area that you may need to seek out help or share with someone. Remember—don't be shy about going to a pastor, church leader, or trusted Christian friend if you realize you have a need.

LOOKING BACK OVER YOUR FIVE DAYS AND CALL TO ACTION,
WRITE DOWN YOUR ANSWERS TO THESE QUESTIONS. IF ANY OF THESE
DON'T APPLY TO YOUR WEEK, SKIP TO THE NEXT QUESTION:

DO YOU HAVE A BIBLICAL OR SPIRITUAL QUESTION
THAT YOU WOULD LIKE TO HAVE ANSWERED?

WAS THERE ANY CONTENT YOU STRUGGLED TO
UNDERSTAND AND WOULD LIKE TO HAVE CLARITY?

DID GOD SHOW YOU ANY TRUTH OR PRINCIPLE FROM THE STUDY THIS WEEK
THAT YOU FEEL YOU NEED TO SHARE WITH SOMEONE IN YOUR LIFE? WHO?

CONSIDERING THE SPECIFIC SCRIPTURES FROM THIS WEEK, DID YOU
HAVE A QUESTION YOU NEED ANSWERED OR SOMETHING YOU FEEL
YOU SHOULD SHARE WITH SOMEONE?

DID SOMETHING SIGNIFICANT HAPPEN IN YOUR WALK WITH GOD THIS
WEEK THAT YOU FEEL YOU NEED TO SHARE WITH SOMEONE AND/OR
ASK THAT PERSON TO PRAY WITH YOU?

HOW WOULD YOU SUM UP YOUR ENGAGEMENT WITH THE
I STILL BELIEVE STUDY THIS WEEK IN ONE OR TWO SENTENCES?

Prayer Time

Take a few minutes to pray for yourself and anyone that God brought to your heart
this week or today in your evaluation. Ask God to open your mind and heart to
receive what he has for you and also for wisdom in any actions you need to take.

Father,

4

YOU ARE GOOD

Sovereignty

Day 22

GOD'S PLAN, PROVISION, AND PURPOSE

s Christians, when we think about the sovereignty of God—his control of all things—our spirit and flesh battle on this topic more than most. We believe God is the Creator and Controller, yet we struggle with letting go of so many things out of fear or stubbornness.

When we add the key ingredient of God's goodness, the battle continues. We read, see, hear, and even experience his goodness, yet we deal with our own interpretation of what we believe to be best in a situation. And then as sinners when we face a difficult circumstance and feel that God is not answering, we can adopt a what-have-you-done-for me-lately attitude. Regardless of spiritual maturity, on some level, this is a daily struggle for us all.

GOD'S PLAN, PROVISION, AND PURPOSE

Romans 8:28 is a very popular and often quoted verse for navigating God's will versus our choices. Let's look at some of the context leading up to that verse.

> FOR IN THIS HOPE WE WERE SAVED. BUT HOPE THAT IS SEEN IS NO HOPE AT ALL. WHO HOPES FOR WHAT THEY ALREADY HAVE? BUT IF WE HOPE FOR WHAT WE DO NOT YET HAVE, WE WAIT FOR IT PATIENTLY. IN

THE SAME WAY, THE SPIRIT HELPS US IN OUR WEAKNESS.
WE DO NOT KNOW WHAT WE OUGHT TO PRAY FOR, BUT
THE SPIRIT HIMSELF INTERCEDES FOR US THROUGH
WORDLESS GROANS. AND HE WHO SEARCHES OUR
HEARTS KNOWS THE MIND OF THE SPIRIT, BECAUSE THE
SPIRIT INTERCEDES FOR GOD'S PEOPLE IN ACCORDANCE
WITH THE WILL OF GOD. AND WE KNOW THAT IN ALL
THINGS GOD WORKS FOR THE GOOD OF THOSE WHO
LOVE HIM, WHO HAVE BEEN CALLED ACCORDING TO HIS
PURPOSE.

- ROMANS 8:24-28

We all suffer and, therefore, long for help that is bigger and better than ourselves and our circumstances. As Christians, we know where to go for that help. We also know that one day we will be delivered eternally from all suffering.

So often, our trials and pain create an inability to even know how to communicate the depth of our feelings and how to find our answers. The amazing truth this passage teaches us about God's goodness is that even when we may not know what to say or ask, his Spirit knows. He offers provision even in our pained stillness, even when silence turns to sobbing.

Because the Spirit is in harmony with the Father and because we are in Christ, we can be in unity with God on our best days and also in the worst possible hours. Jesus interceded for us to provide salvation and now the Spirit intercedes as we walk in that salvation daily.

The Spirit knows our hearts and how to plead for God's children in God's language. What an amazing and miraculous gift we have been given for *any* moment in *any* circumstance!

As we arrive at verse 28, we see that the events of life—all things—that create our deep groaning actually trigger God to work on our behalf. Our calling is three-fold:

- Salvation: freedom from sin and death by the sacrifice of Christ
- Justification: made right with God through the blood of Christ
- Sanctification: daily transformation into the image of Christ

Our ministry to others flows out of these three as both a response and responsibility according to his purpose.

Let's paraphrase today's passage: Nothing comes to a believer except through God's hand, and then the work of his hand is always good. God uses all of life to bring us further and deeper into a relationship with him with the ultimate goal being to populate Heaven.

MISJUDGING MIRACLES

The lone survivor of a shipwreck regained consciousness on the beach of a small, deserted island. Each day he constantly scanned the horizon for ships but saw nothing. He began to cry aloud in desperation for God to save him. After a time, the man decided he needed to build a small shelter for protection from the blazing sun and tropical rain by pulling together brush and branches tied together with strands of seaweed.

One evening just as the sun was setting as he was returning from his daily search for food and water, he came over the last sand dune to see smoke rising up to the sky. As he got closer, he realized flames were lapping up his makeshift home. Crushed and angry, he fell to his knees in disbelief, yelling up at the sky, "God, how could my only shelter catch fire on an island?! Why did you let this happen when I have been crying out to you every day for help?! Why God?! What have I ever done to you?!" With darkness fallen and no way to put out the fire, he lay motionless on the sand as the flames finished their destruction.

Now praying to die, his words were suddenly interrupted by the sound of a blaring horn in the distance. He jumped up and ran to the water, seeing the light of a ship headed toward him. The man began to wave his arms and call out until a spotlight finally hit him. As a small crew came to the shore in a lifeboat, his first question was, "How did you know I was here? How did you find me?" The answer came: "We saw your signal fire and knew there had to be someone stranded way out here."

Our absolute lowest moments in life are sometimes the doorway to a new beginning and a deeper, fresh perspective of our heavenly Father. What may look like a tragedy can turn out to be a transition to a new opportunity. As we see in Romans 8:24-28, the key is to hope, pray, and trust that you will see the goodness of God *in his time*.

"God's sovereignty is something everyone has to grapple with, understanding that he's in control and writing our story. He's the author. I don't know what's going to happen in ten years, but I know God is good, he's in control, and I have to trust him. With the film, all these different topics deal with sovereignty. I also wrote a song called 'The Story's Not Over' because in our journey we learn that nothing is left undone. He uses all things for good. Even though we don't understand the hardship, understanding his goodness in the midst of that is important."

JEREMY CAMP

getting personal

WHAT IS YOUR MOST DIFFICULT STRUGGLE IN TRUSTING THAT GOD IS IN CONTROL? EXPLAIN.

WHAT IS YOUR MOST DIFFICULT STRUGGLE IN BELIEVING THAT GOD IS GOOD AND, THEREFORE, ALWAYS HAS YOUR BEST INTERESTS AT HEART? EXPLAIN.

WHY DO YOU SUPPOSE GOD PROMISED TO MAKE PROVISION FOR US EVEN WHEN WE HAVE NO IDEA WHAT TO DO OR SAY?

HOW MIGHT THE SHIPWRECKED SURVIVOR'S STORY HELP YOU THE NEXT TIME YOU ENCOUNTER A CRISIS?

REFLECT

HOW DOES A BETTER UNDERSTANDING OF GOD'S PLAN AND PROVISION IN ROMANS 8:24-28 HELP YOU TRUST HIM MORE WHEN TRIALS COME? FILL IN THE BLANKS AND THEN USE THIS AS YOUR CLOSING PRAYER:

FATHER, TODAY I AM STRUGGLING WITH:

BECAUSE I LOVE YOU AND AM CALLED ACCORDING TO YOUR PURPOSE, IN THIS SITUATION I AM ASKING YOU TO:

Day 23

BURDENS INTO BLESSINGS

In interviews with Jeremy and Adrienne Camp about the themes of the film *I Still Believe*, they talked about God's sovereignty and also brought up a number of well-known scriptures. One of those verses was Jeremiah 29:11. In that chapter, verse 1 states:

> THIS IS THE TEXT OF THE LETTER THAT THE PROPHET JEREMIAH SENT FROM JERUSALEM TO THE SURVIVING ELDERS AMONG THE EXILES AND TO THE PRIESTS, THE PROPHETS AND ALL THE OTHER PEOPLE NEBUCHADNEZZAR HAD CARRIED INTO EXILE FROM JERUSALEM TO BABYLON.

Through God's plan of correction and restoration, Israel had been taken captive from Jerusalem and forced to live in Babylon. This was obviously a traumatic time in the life of these people. The setting is vital in understanding the context of this verse. Take a look at God's promise to them:

> "FOR I KNOW THE PLANS I HAVE FOR YOU," DECLARES THE LORD, "PLANS TO PROSPER YOU AND NOT TO HARM YOU, PLANS TO GIVE YOU HOPE AND A FUTURE. THEN YOU WILL CALL ON ME AND COME AND

PRAY TO ME, AND I WILL LISTEN TO YOU. YOU WILL
SEEK ME AND FIND ME WHEN YOU SEEK ME WITH ALL
YOUR HEART. I WILL BE FOUND BY YOU," DECLARES
THE LORD, "AND WILL BRING YOU BACK FROM
CAPTIVITY."

- JEREMIAH 29:11-14

LIFE'S COMMAS AND PERIODS

God created the seasons for us to be able to mark changes in our environment through consistent patterns in nature. They are for our benefit,
not his. He does the same thing in our individual lives. As we look back
over the years of our lives, we can see where he marked out starts and
stops for us in distinct places.

Sometimes he brings a new chapter that then leads to the close of an
old one. While other times, he brings an old chapter to a close before
beginning a new one. These situations are much like periods at the end
of sentences.

Sometimes God simply allows changes in our environment, not bringing
anything new, much like commas in sentences. A comma is a change in
the flow of life, while a period is a closing of the old and an opening of
something new. In life, God brings both pauses and periods, but we have
to learn and discern the difference to know his intended purpose.

Each year at midnight on January 1st, when we call out, "Happy New
Year," we have a fresh sense of anticipation and hope that good things
will come with a new start on our calendar. We place a period at the end
of an old year and begin writing a new sentence with the new year. As
we look back over our lives, we see some years that just fade into history
with little to show, while other years are etched into our memory due to
a major blessing or tragedy.

sea·son

/ˈsēzən/

noun

1. a time characterized by a particular circumstance or feature

2. a period of the year characterized by or associated with a particular activity or phenomenon

These life changes that God brings to us, however minimal or massive, a brief resting place or a major shift, cause us to place our hope in him, leaning on verses like Jeremiah 29:11. We pray and hope for seasons of prosperity, for the hope of a blessed future. But we cannot truly appreciate those seasons without first knowing times of trials and suffering.

BURDENS INTO BLESSINGS

In 2003, surfer Bethany Hamilton's life took on a new season when a shark bit off her entire arm just below her shoulder. She shares: "When people ask me what my faith in Christ means to me, I usually answer in just one word: everything! This was true before the shark attack, as well as after. And I truly believe that this faith is a big part of what did get me through it. It helps to know that even when you don't have a clue why something has happened in your life, God has a master plan and is watching over you. It's a tremendous relief to be able to put your trust in God and take the burden off your shoulders." Because of her outspoken faith coupled with the international news carrying her story, she has spent years sharing the Gospel all over the world. Bethany also states that Jeremiah 29:11 is her favorite Bible verse.

Toby never thought he would become the janitor of the elementary school he attended as a child. "When I was younger, I looked at it as a beneath-me kind of job." But at twenty years old with no idea what to do with his life, he took the job. Toby shared,

"I really hated the job at first. I didn't want to be seen as a custodian. When I started, I said, 'I'm just going to take the job to get back on my feet.'"

As the years passed by, the teachers at the school began to urge him to enroll at a local university and take classes around his work schedule. His degree of choice? Elementary school education. A decade later, at thirty years old, Toby graduated and became a teacher at the very same school where he mopped the floors and cleaned the toilets. One teacher said, "He is really great at forming bonds with the kids. That's one of the biggest things a teacher can do to help in a student's success." Toby summarized his story by saying, "Most of the great things in my life started from becoming a custodian."

While Bethany and Toby's stories are vastly different, the common theme is that God can use us right where we are with whatever we have to become whatever he desires for us to be. And the outcome will be for our best, even out of radical changes and difficult seasons.

"JEREMIAH 29:11 SAYS, 'FOR I KNOW THE PLANS I HAVE FOR YOU, PLANS TO PROSPER YOU' AND THEY'RE GOOD THINGS. GOD THINKS OF THE BIGGER PICTURE. LIKE IN THE MOVIE, WE CAN WATCH A CONDENSED VERSION IN AN HOUR AND 50 MINUTE STORY AND SAY, 'OH YEAH, I SEE THE WHOLE PICTURE. BUT WHEN YOU'RE IN THE MIDST OF THOSE TRIALS AND HARDSHIPS, YOU DON'T SEE THAT. YOU CAN'T SEE OR UNDERSTAND GOD'S SOVEREIGNTY OR THE GOODNESS IN THE MIDST OF THAT. IT'S EASY WHEN YOU LOOK BACK IN HINDSIGHT THAT'S 20/20. IF YOU'VE GONE THROUGH SOMETHING HARD, YOU CAN SEE WHAT GOD DID AND SAY, 'I CAN TRUST HIM IN THIS NEW TRIAL BECAUSE I'VE WITNESSED HIS SOVEREIGNTY."

JEREMY CAMP

getting personal

HOW DOES UNDERSTANDING THE CONTEXT THAT GOD HAD ALLOWED HIS PEOPLE TO BE EXILED FROM JERUSALEM TO BABYLON IN CAPTIVITY AFFECT HOW YOU VIEW HIS PROMISE IN JEREMIAH 29:11?

TAKE A MOMENT TO LOOK AT JEREMIAH 29:11-14 AGAIN AND WRITE DOWN THE ACTION PHRASES AND PROMISES YOU SEE?

CONSIDERING JEREMIAH 29:11 AND ALL THE OTHER GREAT SCRIPTURES WE HAVE READ IN THIS JOURNAL, HOW HAS YOUR VIEW OF BEING IN A RELATIONSHIP WITH GOD CHANGED?

HOW DOES THE ANALOGY OF GOD CREATING "PERIODS AND COMMAS"—STARTS, STOPS, AND PAUSES—TO BRING CHANGE HELP YOU BETTER UNDERSTAND HOW HE MAY WORK IN YOUR LIFE?

HOW DO BETHANY AND TOBY'S STORIES INSPIRE YOU IN YOUR OWN JOURNEY TODAY?

BEGIN BY WRITING YOUR FIRST NAME IN EACH OF THE BLANKS, CREATING A PERSONALIZED VERSION OF JEREMIAH 29:11. NOW READ THE WORDS ALOUD AS A REMINDER OF GOD'S PROMISE SPECIFICALLY TO YOU.

FOR I KNOW THE PLANS I HAVE FOR _____

DECLARES THE LORD, "PLANS TO PROSPER

AND NOT TO HARM _____

PLANS TO GIVE _____

HOPE AND A FUTURE. THEN _____

WILL CALL ON ME AND COME AND PRAY TO ME, AND I WILL LISTEN TO_____ .

_____ WILL SEEK ME AND FIND ME WHEN

SEEKS ME WITH ALL_____'S HEART.

I WILL BE FOUND BY_____ .

Day 24

INTENDED EVIL, EVENTUAL GOOD

"In the story of Joseph, one of the greatest stories throughout the Bible, he has these visions that God gave him about his brothers bowing down to him and his family bowing down to him. At first, you're like, 'Man, who is this kid?' You're watching this whole story. But then he's sitting in prison for years. He's faithful and he didn't do anything wrong. I'm sure Joseph is thinking, 'But I had this vision of these great things happening,' as we think, 'Where's the goodness in all this?' But if you look at it in hindsight, what the enemy intended for evil, God meant for good. This had to happen so he could save his family and also an entire nation of people. In the sovereignty of God and his goodness, we ask, 'How does this intertwine together?' And then you finally see the whole picture."

JEREMY CAMP

INTENDED EVIL, EVENTUAL GOOD

The story of Joseph's journey is one of the most intriguing and fascinating of all the accounts in Scripture. Reading his entire story in Genesis, whether for your first time or your hundredth, would be time well spent in connection to the topics in this Journal. Regardless of your familiarity, here are a few highlights:

God had promised Abraham he was going to build a new nation. His first descendant to arrive in Egypt was none other than Joseph. Just as Adam was the first to populate Earth, Joseph, Abraham's great-grandson and the son of Jacob, would begin the fulfillment of God's plan for Israel. But being the deliverer of divine destiny was not at all what this young man was thinking when his journey began.

Joseph had two symbolic dreams where all his brothers bowed down to him, and he told the entire family about them. Imagine for a moment the youngest and favored child in a large family proclaiming that one day they will all kneel before him. Those prophetic dreams became weapons in his brothers' hands. Their jealousy and hatred only grew deeper. While his brothers were all away caring for the family's sheep herds, their father told Joseph to check on them and report back.

Bottom line—Joseph's brothers cooked up a plan to get rid of him after deciding they couldn't kill him. They sold him to a caravan of Ishmaelites on their way to Egypt. Think about Joseph's emotions as he witnessed his own brothers trading him for twenty shekels of silver. Then they all just watched as he disappeared into the distance as a captive.

Through this tale of family dysfunction, we have the unique vantage point of seeing from God's perspective. Through this horrible ordeal for Joseph, God was accomplishing his purposes and fulfilling his promise to Abraham. Through what appears to be a tragic crime will eventually create a national family with God as the King.

After Joseph's enslavement and a stint in prison for a false accusation, in God's timing, he was raised up and rewarded. Pharaoh made him second in command of the nation for saving the country of Egypt from the coming famine.

When Joseph's brothers showed up in Egypt to buy food because he was now grown, they didn't recognize who he was but he certainly knew them. As he was talking to his brothers who had all betrayed him, they knew full well that he had both the right and power to execute them with a snap of his fingers. But the young man proved once again why the Bible continually stated: "The Lord was with Joseph." In Genesis 50:20, he tells his brothers:

> "YOU INTENDED TO HARM ME, BUT GOD INTENDED IT FOR GOOD TO ACCOMPLISH WHAT IS NOW BEING DONE, THE SAVING OF MANY LIVES."

Max Lucado provides his interpretation of Genesis 50:20 by stating, "In God's hands, intended evil becomes eventual good. Joseph told his brothers, using a Hebrew verb that traces its meaning to 'weave' or 'plait.' 'You wove evil,' he was saying, 'but God rewove it together for good.' God, the Master Weaver. He stretches the yarn and intertwines the colors, the ragged twine with the velvet strings, the pains with the pleasures. Nothing escapes His reach. Every king, despot, weather pattern, and molecule are at His command. He passes the shuttle back and forth across the generations, and as He does, a design emerges. Satan weaves; God reweaves."

This is a powerful reminder to us all that when life appears to literally be imploding from within and exploding outside us, God is building something far greater that has been invisible to human eyes. But when finally revealed will be for our best as all the pieces fall into place.

A KICK-IN-THE HEAD MOMENT

Stan Brock was living in the Amazon Rain Forest when a horse kicked him in the head, nearly killing him. Being in such a remote location, there was no doctor nearby. Stan had no choice but to recover on his own. Later, he shared, "It kind of jarred my thinking into, 'Hey, let's bring these doctors a little bit closer than twenty-six days on foot.'"

Stan decided to work towards getting his pilot's license and a small plane to bring medical care to the people in that region. "Instead of taking weeks and weeks, the airplane could get there in just a few hours. If somebody was badly hurt or injured, we could put them in the back of the airplane and take them somewhere for care."

In 1985, Brock started a nonprofit called Remote Area Medical. The volunteer group has provided to hundreds of medical clinics worldwide. Tens of thousands of people, many of them full-time doctors and nurses, have donated their time and expertise to Brock's cause over the years.

For Stan Brock, a literal kick-in-the-head triggered the provision of health care for over half a million people.

This is yet another testimony of how God turn a personal tragedy into a divine treasure to enrich the lives of many.

SATAN WEAVES
God Unweaves

getting personal

DO YOU TEND TO LOOK AT DIFFICULT CIRCUMSTANCES AND QUESTION OF GOD, OR SEARCH OF GOD? EXPLAIN.

REGARDLESS OF YOUR ANSWER AND EXPLANATION, WHAT SORT OF TIPPING POINT DOES IT OR WOULD IT TAKE TO BRING YOU TO THE PLACE WHERE YOU LOOK FOR GOD'S HAND AND EXPECT HIM TO DO SOMETHING GOOD?

HOW DOES UNDERSTANDING THAT JOSEPH'S STORY WAS PART OF A MUCH BIGGER PICTURE ENCOURAGE YOU IN YOUR OWN LIFE AND FAITH JOURNEY?

WHAT ARE YOUR THOUGHTS ABOUT MAX LUCADO'S INTERPRETATION OF GENESIS 50:20: "IN GOD'S HANDS, INTENDED EVIL BECOMES EVENTUAL GOOD"?

IS THERE ANY CIRCUMSTANCE IN YOUR LIFE THAT COULD BECOME YOUR OWN VERSION OF STAN BROCK'S STORY—A TRAGIC MOMENT THAT COULD BE TURNED INTO SOMETHING VALUABLE IN THE HANDS OF GOD TO MINISTER TO OTHERS?

FILL IN THE BLANKS TO CUSTOMIZE GENESIS 50:20 FOR YOURSELF:

GOD, I BELIEVE EVIL IS INTENDED FOR ME TODAY WITH THE SITUATION OF:

BUT I AM ASKING YOU TO CHANGE THE OUTCOME AND BRING ABOUT GOOD BY:

Day 25

LIVING THE GOOD LIFE

In the English language, we can use many words in a wide variety of circumstances. As in the case of our theme this week—You are Good—we use the word "good" to describe Almighty God. But then the connotation quickly changes in situations such as answering with, "No problem. All good." or "The meal was fine. Just good, not great."

The wide range of uses for the word "good' prompts us to take a look at the biblical version of this word. In Genesis 1, when God creates the world, we see him use "good" to describe his completed handiwork light, land, seas, plants, trees, sun, moon, stars, space, creatures in the sea and the air, creatures on the land, the human race and their dominion over creation, Genesis 1:31 puts a bow on everything:

> God saw all that he had made, & it was very good.

In Psalm 73:28, the psalmist states:

> BUT AS FOR ME,
> IT IS GOOD TO
> BE NEAR GOD.
> I HAVE MADE
> THE SOVEREIGN
> LORD MY
> REFUGE; I WILL
> TELL OF ALL
> YOUR DEEDS

In Psalm 84:11:

> "FOR
> THE LORD GOD
> IS A SUN AND
> SHIELD;

THE LORD BESTOWS FAVOR AND HONOR; NO GOOD
THING DOES HE WITHHOLD FROM THOSE WHOSE WALK IS
BLAMELESS."

In Ephesians 2:9-10:

NOT BY WORKS, SO THAT NO ONE CAN BOAST. FOR WE
ARE GOD'S HANDIWORK, CREATED IN CHRIST JESUS TO
DO GOOD WORKS, WHICH GOD PREPARED IN ADVANCE
FOR US TO DO.

In Philippians 2:12-14:

THEREFORE, MY DEAR FRIENDS, AS YOU HAVE ALWAYS
OBEYED—NOT ONLY IN MY PRESENCE, BUT NOW MUCH
MORE IN MY ABSENCE—CONTINUE TO WORK OUT YOUR
SALVATION WITH FEAR AND TREMBLING, FOR IT IS GOD
WHO WORKS IN YOU TO WILL AND TO ACT IN ORDER TO
FULFILL HIS GOOD PURPOSE.

In Mark 10 and Luke 18, Jesus takes issue with a young man using the word "good" out of God's context. A wealthy young man that evidently had a title and power asked Jesus a question in public. "Good teacher, what must I do to inherit eternal life?" Jesus's response is surprising and intriguing as he comes back with a question of his own: "Why do you call me good?" Then he continued, "No one is good—except God alone."

There was then a brief discussion of the commandments with Jesus concluding that the main thing standing between the young man and the kingdom of God was his wealth. Suddenly, the "Good Teacher's" counsel was not very "good." The young man was not willing to let go of earthly possessions and treasures to embrace Heaven, and so he walked away.

The true meaning of good in this world by the standard of Heaven is only applicable in the presence of God. In Matthew Henry's commentary, he states: "When we come to think about our works, we find, to our shame, that much has been very bad; but when God saw his work, all was very good. Good, for it was all just as the Creator would have it to be."

> "I would never think, 'I'm going to sacrifice my son for the good of everyone else.' My idea of what is best wouldn't be the same idea as what God knows is best. That's why we have to trust him. He sent his only son Jesus to die on the cross for the sins of the world so that we can have true forgiveness and a right relationship with him."

JEREMY CAMP

LIVING THE GOOD LIFE

In December of 2006, eighteen-year-old Katie Davis from Tennessee traveled to Uganda for the first time. She had no idea the course of her life would be changed by one mission trip. In 2007, Katie decided to leave her home and plans for college to return to Uganda to teach kindergarten at an orphanage. Soon she was surprised by how many children were sitting on the side of the road or working in the fields during the day. Most of the schools were privately run and required fees for attendance, making an education impossible for most children.

As a response, Katie began a child sponsorship program matching orphaned children with donors to provide for school, supplies, daily meals, medical care, and Christian training. Quickly, Katie had over 150 kids in the program. She also started a similar program to the Karimojong community for over a thousand children.

Katie went on to establish Amazima Ministries International, a non-profit ministry, to meet the physical, emotional, and spiritual needs of orphaned children in Uganda. In the Lugandan language, Amazima means "truth."

By the time Katie was twenty-three years old, she had become the adopted mother of thirteen orphaned girls. In an interview, Katie shared, "People tell me I am brave. People tell me I am strong. People tell me 'good job.' Well, here is the truth of it: I am really not that brave, I am not really that strong, and I am not doing anything spectacular. I am just doing what God called me to do as a follower of him. Feed his sheep, do unto the least of his people." To paraphrase Katie's comments in light of today's subject: The good she does comes from God.

The same spirit clearly seen in the bright eyes and amazing faith of Melissa Camp in *I Still Believe* is also obviously the same spirit that drives Katie Davis. Katie's life is an incredible example of trusting God's sovereign plan and displaying his goodness to "the least of these" that he loves. Such a surrendered life means when her feet hit the floor every morning, her life has divine purpose and meaning. ■

TRULY I TELL YOU, WHATEVER YOU DID FOR ONE OF THE LEAST OF THESE, YOU DID FOR *me*

getting personal

WE SEE IN GENESIS 1 THAT GOD STOPPED, LOOKED AT HIS CREATION, AND CALLED IT GOOD. WHAT DOES HIS RESPONSE SAY TO YOU IN THE BUSY DAYS OF YOUR LIFE?

IN THE LIST OF SCRIPTURES USING THE WORD "GOOD," WHAT DO YOU FEEL IS THE COMMON THREAD IN ALL THOSE VERSES?

IN PSALM 84:11, WE READ THE PHRASE, "NO GOOD THING DOES HE WITHHOLD FROM THOSE WHOSE WALK IS BLAMELESS," HOW DOES THIS ENCOURAGE YOUR PERCEPTION OF GOD'S DESIRE TO BLESS YOU?

WHEN THINKING ABOUT THE STORY OF JESUS AND THE WEALTHY MAN, WHY DO SO MANY OF US CONTINUE TO STRUGGLE WITH THE IDEA THAT MONEY, POWER, AND FAME ARE "GOOD" WHEN THE BIBLE SO OFTEN WARNS OF THEIR DANGERS?

WHAT INSPIRED YOU THE MOST ABOUT KATIE DAVIS'S STORY? WHY?

FILL IN THE BLANKS USING EPHESIANS 2:9-11 WITH THE MINISTRY AND GIFTING YOU BELIEVE GOD HAS GIVEN YOU TO USE FOR HIM:

FOR [I] AM GOD'S HANDIWORK, CREATED IN CHRIST JESUS TO DO:

WHICH GOD PREPARED IN ADVANCE FOR [ME] TO DO."

Day 26

THE CLAUS CASE

We have all heard the stories of people being asked if they believe they are going to Heaven. The answers often come back: "Well, I think so because I am a good person" or "Yes, because God knows I am a good person."

Very early in life, many people pick up on the false idea that God and the hope of Heaven are connected to us being "good enough." Salvation is somehow based on our merit. Of course, the real issue here is we are judging using our flawed and sinful human scale of goodness. The idea that behavior is the gatekeeper to Heaven is born out of religion and the many belief systems of the ages created by man trying to "find God."

THE CLAUS CASE

Anytime you watch children being interviewed before Christmas that are asked if they have been good or bad during the past year, they know the "Santa standard" well. They typically swallow hard, think for a moment, believe for the best, and say they have been good. Why?

Because they already understand that their behavior is the key to the amount of blessing on Christmas morning, based on what they have been told since they could remember.

But even kids can often sense that something is not quite right with this system. "Well, I know I have done some bad things, but I really hope the good outweighs the bad, so I can get what I want." One of the strongest human fears of a child is being left out of the blessing line from any cosmic creature whether that be Santa, the Easter Bunny, the Tooth Fairy. Then as adults, we can easily associate the same principle with any god in any religion.

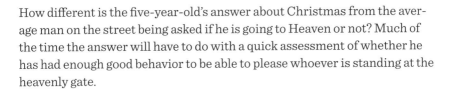

How different is the five-year-old's answer about Christmas from the average man on the street being asked if he is going to Heaven or not? Much of the time the answer will have to do with a quick assessment of whether he has had enough good behavior to be able to please whoever is standing at the heavenly gate.

What we have laid out thus far is a case for how we have come to treat the concept of a god or even *the* God like a supernatural Santa Claus. In any religion, you either believe in him, or you don't believe in him, but if you do, then your behavior alone determines your rewards here on earth and beyond. Life is lived hoping the good will override your spot on the naughty list and get you into the right afterlife.

This brand of belief is dependent solely on our own efforts. But if we choose to believe in a higher power, then why would we not also trust that he would offer some sort of help to gain access into his kingdom? What kind of god is just a doorkeeper to some celestial home, judging who can and cannot come in? That actually sounds more like a bouncer at a nightclub than a supernatural power!

THE REALITY OF THE GOSPEL

So to honestly and effectively present the belief we read about in the Bible, we have to look into the Word of God. Here are a few points of evidence found in Romans:

"THERE IS NO ONE RIGHTEOUS, NOT EVEN ONE; THERE IS NO ONE WHO UNDERSTANDS; THERE IS NO ONE WHO SEEKS GOD."

- ROMANS 3:10-11

FOR ALL HAVE SINNED AND FALL SHORT OF THE
GLORY OF GOD, AND ALL ARE JUSTIFIED FREELY BY
HIS GRACE THROUGH THE REDEMPTION THAT CAME BY
CHRIST JESUS.

- ROMANS 3:22-24

BUT GOD DEMONSTRATES HIS OWN LOVE FOR US IN
THIS: WHILE WE WERE STILL SINNERS, CHRIST DIED
FOR US.

- ROMANS 5:8

FOR THE WAGES OF SIN IS DEATH, BUT THE GIFT OF
GOD IS ETERNAL LIFE IN CHRIST JESUS OUR LORD.

- ROMANS 6:23

Clearly our behavior cannot be the key to the gates of Heaven. We are all on the naughty list. But God knew we could never become good on our own. That is why he offers us his righteousness through a relationship with his Son, Jesus Christ because of "his own love for us" as 5:8 states. The "gift of God" from 6:23 is offered because of his goodness, not ours. That gift proves *his* goodness, compassion, and kindness can overcome and overrule all our bad behavior, no matter what level of "good or bad" we are.

THE GIFT OF GOD IS OFFERED
because of his goodness

> **"Because God is also omniscient, he literally knows everything. I think that should comfort us like, 'Yeah! That's my God! That's how big he is.' In the movie, I love the planetarium scene. It's really breathtaking as you see them looking up at the stars and then Melissa says, 'Look at all these vast amounts of stars and the galaxies and the trillions of stars. God is huge and he knows my name.' That's where we have to rest in the beautiful picture of God's vastness. That's how personally and intimately acquainted he is with us."**

JEREMY CAMP

God indeed does want to be personally and intimately acquainted with us. Here is a brief and simple presentation of the Gospel of the good, good Father with Scripture references:

Innocent of sin, Jesus took our punishment by expressing his love, giving his own life for each of us. John 15:13 states, *"Greater love has no one than this: to lay down one's life for one's friends."* Each person must decide whether or not to accept Jesus' death as the replacement for his own. God, in his great love, gives you the freedom to choose.

In John 14:6 Jesus said, *"I am the way and the truth and the life. No one comes to the Father except through me."* Once you have prayed and agreed he is your Savior, (Romans 10:9-10) you are a new person (2 Corinthians 5:17). With your sin forgiven and your past forgotten by God (Hebrews 8:12), you can now live inside his forgiveness (Galatians 2:20). You are saved by his grace (Ephesians 2:8-9) and freed in his eyes from past mistakes to live a life of serving him and others in his power (Colossians 1:28-29).

God's sovereignty is on full display in the Gospel. He took care of every detail of salvation, knowing we are helpless on our own. Forgiveness, redemption, grace, adoption, freedom, and access to his authority are available to anyone who will call on his name. Only the One who creates and controls all things can offer us everything he has. ■

getting personal

WHY DO YOU SUPPOSE THE IDEA THAT OUR GOODNESS CAN GET US INTO HEAVEN HAS BEEN PREVALENT IN OUR CULTURE FOR SO LONG?

WHY DO YOU SUPPOSE PEOPLE WILL DECIDE TO RELY ON THEIR OWN EFFORTS OR MERITS TO ENTER HEAVEN?

HOW DOES THE SANTA CLAUS ANALOGY MAKE SENSE, ESPECIALLY WHEN COMPARED TO THE WORLD'S RELIGIONS TEACHING THE CONNECTION BETWEEN BELIEF AND BEHAVIOR?

DID YOU LEARN ANYTHING NEW TODAY ABOUT THE REALITY OF
THE GOSPEL? EXPLAIN.

BELOW IS A VERY SIMPLE WAY TO TALK ABOUT YOUR FAITH—YOUR
OWN STORY OF WHAT THE LORD HAS DONE FOR YOU. IN THREE
TO FOUR SENTENCES FOR EACH POINT, WRITE DOWN:

MY LIFE BEFORE CHRIST WAS:

I CAME TO KNOW CHRIST BY/THROUGH:

MY RELATIONSHIP WITH JESUS CHANGED MY LIFE BY:

TODAY, GOD IS AT WORK IN MY LIFE BY/THROUGH:

AFTER YOU WRITE OUT YOUR TESTIMONY, GO OVER IT AND
MEMORIZE YOUR STORY TO BE ABLE TO QUICKLY AND CONCISELY
SHARE YOUR FAITH WITH ANYONE.

Day 27

CALL TO ACTION

As you have now come to the close of your fourth week, have you found that you are going deeper in how you process the content? Is the importance of your personal application becoming clearer to you as you work through the week? When we realize we are growing spiritually and getting closer to Christ, there is a synergy created as we learn to go deeper into our maturity. Moving into today, devise your plan for application and living out what God has shown you.

As a Christ-follower, God has a distinct calling on your life. He has a purpose planned for you. While we are all aware of 3D technology, here are three Ds to watch for as you grow in your relationship with Jesus:

THE FIRST IS DISCOVER— DISCOVER YOUR PASSION

What excites you in ministry and reaching people? What do you take part in that you know glorifies God? God has placed an innate passion in your heart that is directly connected to his heart. When you have the opportunity to engage in that activity, you feel at peace, feel at home, with a deep sense of divine satisfaction and personal gratification. You have the feeling of "this is what I was made to do." If you have not discovered this yet, as you get closer to Christ, he will bring the passion out of you in his time and his way.

THE SECOND IS DEFINE—DEFINE YOUR CALLING

How does God want you to use your passion, gift, skills, or talents in the world? *Who* can you reach with them?

Where can you best use them? *When* can you best use them? The vehicle for which you use your passion for ministry to others is your calling. If you pray and seek what God is calling you to do, whether one hour a week or full-time or anywhere in between, he will show you because he is the one who has called you.

THE THIRD IS DEVELOP—DEVELOP YOUR MINISTRY.

When your passion and calling are mixed with your obedience, then God's power and presence connect, and lives will be changed. Your ministry will be something you could never do on your own, only something you and God can do together. You both will look over your partnership of reaching hearts and call it "good."

Walking through this three-step process is very much like pouring any liquid through a funnel. The process of pouring directs the liquid *exactly* where it needs to go with simple effort and no waste. It's all in. You pour who you are into God's kingdom out of your created purpose as he blesses. He's all in!

> YOUR PASSION IS FUNNELED INTO YOUR CALLING AND YOUR CALLING IS FUNNELED INTO YOUR MINISTRY.

WHAT BIBLE VERSE OR PASSAGE DID YOU MOST CONNECT WITH THIS
WEEK? NEXT, WRITE DOWN WHY YOU FEEL THAT MESSAGE CONNECTED
AND THE IMPACT IT HAD ON YOU.

WHAT WAS ONE TRUTH OR PRINCIPLE YOU
BELIEVE GOD SPOKE TO YOU THIS PAST WEEK?

HAS GOD IMPRESSED ANY NEW THING ON YOU
THAT YOU BELIEVE HE WANTS YOU TO BEGIN?

HAS GOD IMPRESSED ANYTHING ON YOU THAT YOU
BELIEVE HE WANTS YOU TO SURRENDER TO HIM?

WAS THERE ANY RELATIONSHIP IN YOUR LIFE THAT YOU SENSED GOD WANTS YOU TO TAKE ACTION?

A CHRISTIAN FRIEND YOU NEED TO ENCOURAGE?

A NON-CHRISTIAN YOU NEED TO MINISTER TO?

GOD'S WILL

WHAT IS ONE TRUTH YOU LEARNED ABOUT GOD'S SOVEREIGNTY?

WHAT ONE STEP OF OBEDIENCE DOES GOD WANT
YOU TO TAKE TO CARRY OUT HIS PLAN FOR YOU?

GOD'S WILL

WRITE YOUR PRAYER HERE

father,

Day 28

PREP & PRAY

I f you are using this Journal in connection with a small group study ... This should be the day of your small group meeting for the *I Still Believe* study. We want to give you the grace and space for two things:

1. If you need to catch up on any day that you may have missed, this time will allow you to be sure you engage fully with *all* the content. If you were pressed for time on any particular day, use this opportunity to go back and review.

2. We want to give you an opportunity to prepare for your group meeting so you can offer all you need to contribute.

Remember:

- TRANSFORMATION OVER INFORMATION.
- EXPERIENCE OVER ATTENDANCE.
- CONTRIBUTION AND INTERACT.
- SHARE AND ENCOURAGE.
- BE AVAILABLE AND OBEDIENT.
- GROW AND GIVE.

Preparation for Your Small Group Meeting

LOOKING BACK OVER YOUR FIVE DAYS AND CALL TO ACTION, WRITE
DOWN YOUR ANSWERS TO THESE QUESTIONS. IF ANY OF THESE
DON'T APPLY TO YOUR WEEK, SKIP TO THE NEXT QUESTION:

DO YOU HAVE A QUESTION YOU WOULD WANT TO RAISE TO THE GROUP
LEADER FOR FURTHER CLARIFICATION OR DISCUSSION?

WAS THERE ANY CONTENT YOU STRUGGLED TO UNDERSTAND AND
WOULD LIKE TO HAVE CLARITY? (REMEMBER—GETTING YOUR QUESTION
ANSWERED COULD HELP SOMEONE ELSE.)

DID GOD SHOW YOU ANY TRUTH OR PRINCIPLE FROM THE STUDY THIS
WEEK THAT YOU FEEL YOU WOULD LIKE TO SHARE WITH THE GROUP?

CONSIDERING THE SPECIFIC SCRIPTURES FROM THIS WEEK, DID YOU HAVE A
QUESTION OR COMMENT YOU WOULD WANT TO SHARE WITH THE GROUP?

DID SOMETHING SIGNIFICANT HAPPEN IN YOUR WALK WITH GOD THIS
WEEK THAT YOU WOULD LIKE TO SHARE OR REQUEST PRAYER FOR?

HOW WOULD YOU SUM UP YOUR ENGAGEMENT WITH THE *I STILL
BELIEVE* STUDY THIS WEEK IN ONE OR TWO SENTENCES?

Pray for Your Small Group

Take a few minutes to pray for your group meeting. Pray for:

• Your leader

• Each member

• Any ongoing requests of your members

• God to open your mind and heart to receive what he has for you

• Wisdom in what you need to contribute to your group's dynamic

If you are using this Journal for your personal study only

Today allows you the opportunity to catch up on the content if needed. The questions below are designed to help you evaluate your experience this week, as well as indicate any area that you may need to seek out help or share with someone. Remember—don't be shy about going to a pastor, church leader, or trusted Christian friend if you realize you have a need.

LOOKING BACK OVER YOUR FIVE DAYS AND CALL TO ACTION,
WRITE DOWN YOUR ANSWERS TO THESE QUESTIONS. IF ANY OF THESE
DON'T APPLY TO YOUR WEEK, SKIP TO THE NEXT QUESTION:

DO YOU HAVE A BIBLICAL OR SPIRITUAL QUESTION
THAT YOU WOULD LIKE TO HAVE ANSWERED?

WAS THERE ANY CONTENT YOU STRUGGLED TO
UNDERSTAND AND WOULD LIKE TO HAVE CLARITY?

DID GOD SHOW YOU ANY TRUTH OR PRINCIPLE FROM THE STUDY THIS WEEK
THAT YOU FEEL YOU NEED TO SHARE WITH SOMEONE IN YOUR LIFE? WHO?

CONSIDERING THE SPECIFIC SCRIPTURES FROM THIS WEEK, DID YOU
HAVE A QUESTION YOU NEED ANSWERED OR SOMETHING YOU FEEL
YOU SHOULD SHARE WITH SOMEONE?

DID SOMETHING SIGNIFICANT HAPPEN IN YOUR WALK WITH GOD THIS
WEEK THAT YOU FEEL YOU NEED TO SHARE WITH SOMEONE AND/OR
ASK THAT PERSON TO PRAY WITH YOU?

HOW WOULD YOU SUM UP YOUR ENGAGEMENT WITH THE
I STILL BELIEVE STUDY THIS WEEK IN ONE OR TWO SENTENCES?

Prayer Time

Take a few minutes to pray for yourself and anyone that God brought to your heart
this week or today in your evaluation. Ask God to open your mind and heart to
receive what he has for you and also for wisdom in any actions you need to take.

father,

5

YOU ARE
FOR ME

Commitment

Day 29

JOY VS. HAPPINESS

In the *I Still Believe* film, there are moments of incredible blessing and great joy, along with gut-wrenching scenes of deep sadness and overwhelming grief. While the timeline of every human life is dramatically different, we will all eventually find ourselves in these two extremes. Along our journeys in this fallen world, the unfortunate fact remains that we cannot escape suffering.

In the Christian life comprehending joy in trials is a very important, yet often misunderstood topic. In just two powerful sentences, James 1:2-3 paints the picture for us of what a relationship with Christ offers for this deeply human struggle.

CONSIDER IT PURE JOY, MY BROTHERS AND SISTERS, WHENEVER YOU FACE TRIALS OF MANY KINDS, BECAUSE YOU KNOW THAT THE TESTING OF YOUR FAITH PRODUCES PERSEVERANCE. LET PERSEVERANCE FINISH ITS WORK SO THAT YOU MAY BE MATURE AND COMPLETE, NOT LACKING ANYTHING.

Joy is often confused as just a different version of happiness. That is exactly why so many people think how impossible it would be to have joy during a crisis. But James did *not* say, "Be happy whenever you face trials." As with all Scripture, his word choice was very intentional. Here are some reasons:

• Happiness is like a thermometer fluctuating at the moment, while joy is a thermostat providing a steady constant.

- Happiness struggles to be present in problems, while joy is at its best when trouble comes.
- Happiness is a temporary state of mind, while joy is a mindset.
- Happiness is based on conditions, while biblical joy, like Christ's love, is *un*conditional.

James defines joy as not removing the negative circumstances from our lives. Rather, we embrace them as opportunities to experience something eternal, allowing God to strengthen our faith and create spiritual maturity.

But let's take this concept even deeper: the joy found in a relationship with Jesus has everything to do with remaining in his presence when suffering shows up at our door and storms into our house, especially when we didn't see it coming. Whatever life throws at us, *joy* is always available, even when *happiness* may be a distant memory at the time. For the Camps, a cancer diagnosis challenged their every ounce of happiness, but Melissa exuded a supernatural peace and joy throughout her struggles.

James tells us that choosing joy results in maturity and completeness in Christ, even going to the point of adding the phrase, "not lacking anything." If everything we need is available, we don't have to lack anything.

Trials can become the fuel that drives us to experience a deeper relationship with Jesus.

> **"Commitment for me in my relationship with the Lord goes way beyond just saying, 'I believe in God'. A lot of people say, 'I believe in God, that he exists.' But that's not being committed to him. It's saying, 'I make him Lord of my life.' The primary thing that I serve in life is God. That's being committed to his ways, committed to his Word, dedicated to him—always."**

JEREMY CAMP

MESS OR MASTERPIECE?

A middle school boy came home, threw his backpack on the floor, and slumped down into a chair. His mom, who was standing in the kitchen, asked, "So you want to talk about it?"

He immediately began blurting out through tears how everything in his world was falling apart. The girl he liked was mad at him, and he didn't know why. He failed a test that day he had studied hard for. He couldn't possibly make the basketball team because the other guys were so good.

When he finished with his long list, the mom reached under the cabinet and grabbed some cooking oil. "I'm so sorry about what you're going through. Would you like a glass of this?" The boy shot back, "What? No!" She then went to the pantry, grabbed some flour, and asked, "Okay, what about a big bowl of this?" The boy, confused, walked into the kitchen. "Mom! Are you feeling okay?"

Ignoring his question, she went on to ask if he'd like some raw eggs? Vanilla extract? Some sugar? Finally suspicious, the son asked, "Alright, I give. What's your point?"

"Son, all these individual ingredients, no one would want to eat by themselves, and most would taste really bad alone, maybe even make you sick. But when I mix all these up and bake a cake, you see—and taste—what happens when you choose to make the best out of a lot of yucky things." ∎

see what happens

when you make the

best out of yucky

things.

getting personal

REFLECT

EXPLAIN IN YOUR OWN WORDS WHY JAMES MIGHT HAVE CHOSEN
THE WORD "JOY" INSTEAD OF "HAPPINESS"?

WHY DO YOU THINK GOD ALLOWS OUR FAITH TO BE TESTED WHEN
HE ALREADY KNOWS OUR HEARTS AND MINDS?

HOW DO YOUR PRAYERS DIRECTLY IMPACT YOUR LEVEL OF JOY IN
A TRIAL AND, ULTIMATELY, YOUR PERSEVERANCE?

THINKING ABOUT THE STORY OF THE MOM'S LESSON FOR HER
SON, WRITE DOWN ONE SITUATION IN YOUR LIFE WHERE YOU
HAVE SEEN GOD CREATE A MASTERPIECE FROM A MESS.

IN THAT SITUATION, WHAT CREATED THE TURNING POINT FOR GOD TO WORK? WHAT DID YOU DO? WHAT DID HE DO?

IN CLOSING TODAY, USING THE WORDS OF JAMES 1:2 IN THE FIRST BLANK BELOW, WRITE YOUR FIRST NAME. IN THE SECOND BLANK, WRITE DOWN A CURRENT TRIAL YOU ARE GOING THROUGH.

CONSIDER IT PURE JOY, _____

WHENEVER YOU FACE _____

"JESUS, I GIVE YOU THIS SITUATION. HELP ME TO PASS THIS TEST OF MY FAITH. PLEASE PRODUCE PERSEVERANCE IN ME AS I WALK THROUGH THIS—NOT GOING AROUND IT OR RUNNING AWAY FROM IT. FINISH YOUR WORK SO THAT I MAY BE MATURE AND COMPLETE IN YOU, NOT LACKING ANYTHING. I CHOOSE TO RECEIVE WHAT YOU WANT ME TO HAVE FROM YOUR HAND AND HEART. IN JESUS'S NAME, AMEN."

CONSIDER USING THIS SAME JAMES 1 EXERCISE AND PRAYER ANY TIME YOU EXPERIENCE A TRIAL.

Day 30

THE FOLLOW-ME FACTOR

Throughout the Gospels, there is a short phrase repeated consistently that Jesus said to many: "Come and follow me." Through every generation, Jesus offers that invitation to all people. Those who have decided to follow him have simply answered that same call by his Spirit in their hearts. There is no other way to salvation outside of receiving his invitation.

But a very crucial truth to embrace is that while Jesus's offer stands every day for the rest of our lives, we still have a moment-by-moment choice of walking with him or going our own way. It is no longer a matter of eternal salvation but a question of day-to-day obedience.

In our western culture, if someone we know says, "Hey, come on, let's go. Follow me," our tendency is to ask a bevy of questions: *Where exactly are we going? How long will we be gone? How much money will I need? What should I wear?* That same mindset creates a religion where when Jesus says, "Follow me," the response is often: *First, I want to know where you are taking me? Is it going to be somewhere I don't like? Are we going to do something I won't like? What time will we get back?*

We live in a time when many who say they are Christians struggle to truly follow Christ. They want Heaven when they die and God's blessings here and now, but don't want anything difficult asked of them. The great problem with this paradigm is the only two guarantees we have in following Jesus is, one, we will go to Heaven to be with him, and two, he will be with us in this life.

When Jesus asks us to follow him, his invitation provides no advance plan and no immediate direction. We must follow in faith, not by sight. We must follow out of love, not in fear. We go with him out of a commitment of belief, not simply to comply out of duty. But when we follow, we will always be in the best and safest place because we are in his hands and his will.

Following James 1:2-3 where we read about joy experienced through trials to persevere to maturity, James continues to challenge believers about the importance of walking daily in faith and commitment.

> IF ANY OF YOU LACKS WISDOM, YOU SHOULD ASK
> GOD, WHO GIVES GENEROUSLY TO ALL WITHOUT
> FINDING FAULT, AND IT WILL BE GIVEN TO YOU. BUT
> WHEN YOU ASK, YOU MUST BELIEVE AND NOT
> DOUBT, BECAUSE THE ONE WHO DOUBTS IS LIKE
> A WAVE OF THE SEA, BLOWN AND TOSSED BY THE
> WIND.
>
> - JAMES 1:4-6

We all know the feeling of "going back and forth" in any important decision or response to a crisis. James encourages us that God is ready to give us his wisdom if we will simply believe, ask, and then listen for and obey when he answers. The One who walked on water in the storm can keep us steady and not "blown and tossed" about in a sea of indecision.

THE MAZE, THE MAP, AND THE MAKER

Centuries ago, an extremely wealthy man lived in a spacious castle near a small village. His property covered thousands upon thousands of acres. His vaults were full of gold and silver. One day the man walked into the town square and announced he had built a giant maze on his property that stretched out over several hundred acres with very high walls. The caveat was this: He had placed much of his wealth in the center of the maze and anyone who could get to it could have everything.

Because the villagers were very poor, many people packed up some supplies, said goodbye to their families, and set out to find the treasure. After several weeks of no word, a few people began to emerge from the maze, barely finding their way out alive. They told tales of some dying, some falling ill, and others going insane from being hopelessly lost.

One day, a young man stood at the entrance contemplating his own journey, when he heard a voice behind him ask, "So, are you going in alone?" Startled, he turned and saw a stranger behind him. "Oh no, I am afraid. Many have lost their lives in there, and I would surely die also." The man looked deep into his eyes and said, "Son, I built that maze. I have the map. I know every corner and turn. You can stay close and I will lead you straight to the treasure—if you will trust and choose to follow me."

Life presents a maze of physical, mental, emotional, and spiritual walls that can make us feel lost and closed-in. But God made us, along with the world in which we live, wrote the map for life, will lead us through anything we come up against, and at the end of the journey leads us to Heaven.

IF YOU DON'T KNOW WHAT YOU'RE DOING, PRAY TO THE FATHER. HE LOVES TO HELP. YOU'LL GET HIS HELP, AND WON'T BE CONDESCENDED TO WHEN YOU ASK FOR IT. ASK BOLDLY, BELIEVINGLY, WITHOUT A SECOND THOUGHT.

- JAMES 1:5 MSG

"Some of the hardest things that Jeremy and I have had to walk through are things people have said or done that hurts so deeply. And so there's a level of commitment to working out those things in our hearts that when offenses come and difficult things come, that we have to commit to walking in forgiveness and walking in love and really choosing to keep moving forward."

ADRIENNE CAMP

getting personal

TODAY, APPROACH THESE OPEN-ENDED SENTENCES AS A DIALOGUE WITH GOD.

FATHER, THE WALLS I FEEL THAT ARE CLOSING IN ON ME TODAY ARE COMING FROM:

FATHER, I NEED YOUR WISDOM TODAY TO:

FATHER, BEING HONEST WITH YOU TODAY, MY DOUBTS IN THIS STRUGGLE ARE:

FATHER, I BELIEVE I CAN CHOOSE TO WALK IN FAITH AND FOLLOW YOU
TODAY BECAUSE:

FATHER, HERE IS MY PRAYER TO HAND OVER MY BURDENS AND CAST
MY CARES ON YOU TODAY:

Day 31

THOSE WHO LOVE

In *I Still Believe*, both Jeremy and Melissa had several points where either could have made a decision to end their relationship with the other or with God. But when the struggle and stress rose to the highest level, their faith, individually and together, made the hard call to push forward through the flames, no matter how hot the fire became. This is not because they were somehow given supernatural powers, but rather because they placed all their belief and commitment in their love for an almighty God and one another.

Going farther into the first chapter of James, he expands on the promises God offers as we endure life's trials.

BLESSED IS THE ONE
WHO PERSEVERES UNDER
TRIAL BECAUSE, HAVING
STOOD THE TEST, THAT
PERSON WILL RECEIVE THE
CROWN OF LIFE THAT THE
LORD HAS PROMISED
TO THOSE WHO LOVE
HIM.

- JAMES 1:12

Take a look at the last line again for the reason to even persevere and stand the test at all—to love him.

THRIVING IN THE FIRE

Giant sequoias found in massive forests in the Pacific Northwest are the largest trees on the earth. Some are believed to be as old as 3,000 years. But a very surprising fact about these gigantic trees is that without fire they cannot continue to reproduce. Forest fires create three factors that these trees require.

First, fire heats the cones in the mature sequoia trees, causing the cones to open and literally pour seeds onto the ground. Secondly, fires burn up everything piled on the forest floor, clearing the way for the seeds to bury in the now bare soil. Lastly, fires create holes in the canopy of the forest, allowing in light and water for the seedlings.

Sequoia seed germination naturally occurs best in fire-burned, mineral-rich soils. Sequoia seedlings are far more likely to survive where fire has burned the hottest, literally birthed among the ashes. The largest, tallest, strongest trees on the planet need fire to thrive.

While it can be difficult to admit as Christians, for us to grow strong, mature, and complete in our faith, we, too, need the "fires of life" to thrive. Unfortunately, we grow the deepest down in the valley, not up on the mountain. We get closer to the Lord in seasons of burden, not blessing. So many miraculous testimonies of where God has moved mightily are from those who come through fire.

PUSHING AWAY PROVIDENTIAL PAIN

C.S. Lewis wrote, "Pain insists upon being attended to. God whispers to us in our pleasures, speaks in our consciences, but shouts in our pains. It is his megaphone to rouse a deaf world."

Our western culture has long been fixated on comfort. From cars to furniture to clothing to technology, we desire anything that will make our lives better, easier, and faster. Because of that focus, any discomfort, especially suffering, is avoided at all costs, even to the point that many Christians perceive trials as God somehow removing himself from them or even punishing them.

To the other side, depression, anxiety, addictions of all kinds, violent responses, and suicide occur at alarming rates. So we have become a culture of extremes. We demand a level of comfort no people in history have ever known, so we also desire to dull any pain we feel.

As Christians, we come from an amazing legacy of committed, dedicated people who created a testimony through unimaginable circumstances. Not superheroes, but normal folks with faith in an all-powerful God. When

we are tempted to give up during the hard things life can bring and forfeit the opportunity to honor and serve Christ. May we be reminded that: We were given an opportunity to believe...

Because Abraham didn't say, "Sorry, I don't do road trips."
Because Moses didn't say, "Sorry, I don't do Pharaohs."
Because Noah didn't say, "Sorry, I don't do arks."
Because David didn't say, "Sorry, I don't do battles."
Because Mary didn't say, "Sorry, I don't do virgin births."
Because Peter didn't say, "Sorry, I don't do preaching."
Because Paul didn't say, "Sorry, I don't do prisons."
Because Jesus didn't say, "Sorry, I don't do crosses."

"The word that comes to mind for me when I think of commitment is steadfastness. When something really has a hold of your heart, even through ups and downs, there's a level of commitment, like you're anchored in, no matter what. It's a decision that's made, not based on your emotions or circumstances, but a promise. No matter what, you're going to stick it out."

ADRIENNE CAMP

getting personal

REFLECT

WHEN HAS SOMETHING GOOD BEEN BIRTHED OUT OF ASHES IN YOUR LIFE?

CONSIDERING THE FACTS ABOUT THE GIANT SEQUOIA TREES, WHEN HAS A "FIRE" IN YOUR LIFE ACTUALLY HELPED YOU THRIVE IN A WAY YOU OTHERWISE WOULDN'T?

WHAT ARE YOUR THOUGHTS REGARDING THE C.S. LEWIS QUOTE ABOUT GOD'S WHISPERS AND SHOUTS?

IS THERE ANY AREA OF YOUR LIFE WHERE YOU ARE TRYING TO PUSH AWAY PAIN THAT GOD MIGHT BE ATTEMPTING TO USE FOR YOUR GROWTH AND HIS GLORY?

IS THERE ANY AREA OF YOUR LIFE WHERE YOU ARE INSISTING ON COMFORT OVER WHAT GOD MIGHT BE CALLING YOU TO DO?

ARE THERE ANY "SORRY, I DON'T DO (BLANK)" STAND-OFFS WITH GOD IN YOUR LIFE?

IS THERE A TRIAL YOU ARE IN RIGHT NOW WHERE YOU ARE STRUGGLING TO PERSEVERE?

FATHER, TODAY I SURRENDER_____
TO YOU. I ASK YOU TO GIVE ME THE STRENGTH TO PERSEVERE BY

_____.

Day 32

HEARING FROM THE HEART

By the time Jeremy asked Melissa to marry him, she already knew how much he loved her and how committed he was to her life and the Lord. Why? Because of the many gestures of love, service, and sacrifice he had already done for her. The story told through *I Still Believe* is not about what the Camps *said* they believed, but about what they actually did, how they put feet to their faith. Words and confessions became actions and sacrifices. They chose to live out their commitment to Christ with their relationship being one of the primary vessels.

Continuing forward in the first chapter of James, he keeps up his strong challenge regarding the end goal of belief. Today is a short but potent passage.

DO NOT MERELY LISTEN TO THE WORD, AND SO DECEIVE YOURSELVES. DO WHAT IT SAYS.

- JAMES 1:22

Very straightforward, right? Where did James get this direct approach to what we do with God's Word? The answer is found in the consistent message of Jesus's teaching. Here is just one example:

"THEREFORE EVERYONE WHO HEARS THESE WORDS OF MINE AND PUTS THEM

INTO PRACTICE IS LIKE A WISE MAN WHO BUILT HIS HOUSE
ON THE ROCK. THE RAIN CAME DOWN, THE STREAMS ROSE,
AND THE WINDS BLEW AND BEAT AGAINST THAT HOUSE;
YET IT DID NOT FALL, BECAUSE IT HAD ITS FOUNDATION
ON THE ROCK. BUT EVERYONE WHO HEARS THESE WORDS
OF MINE AND DOES NOT PUT THEM INTO PRACTICE IS LIKE
A FOOLISH MAN WHO BUILT HIS HOUSE ON SAND. THE
RAIN CAME DOWN, THE STREAMS ROSE, AND THE WINDS
BLEW AND BEAT AGAINST THAT HOUSE, AND IT FELL WITH
A GREAT CRASH."

- MATTHEW 7:24-27

Jesus said that both men heard his words. So what was the difference? One applied them to action and the other didn't. To echo James, the foolish man merely listened to the word, deceived himself, and did not do what it said.

The foundational principle here is once we read a truth in God's Word or hear it taught to us, we become responsible for that word. We become stewards of God's Word in our lives. We then make a choice—do what he says or ignore to go our own way.

Crowds of people came to hear Jesus speak that never became his disciples. They heard his words and went on with their lives unchanged. The same is true today. Crowds of people attend church every week and hear messages from God's Word that never become Jesus's disciples. Both Jesus and James make it clear that hearing is just step one. Step two is to then live out the truth heard. That is the end goal of belief, faith, and commitment to Christ—a transformed life in word and action. Jesus himself set that example for us.

FOR THIS REASON HE HAD TO BE MADE LIKE THEM, FULLY
HUMAN IN EVERY WAY, IN ORDER THAT HE MIGHT
BECOME A MERCIFUL AND FAITHFUL HIGH PRIEST IN

SERVICE TO GOD, AND THAT HE MIGHT
MAKE ATONEMENT FOR THE SINS OF THE
PEOPLE. BECAUSE HE HIMSELF SUFFERED
WHEN HE WAS TEMPTED, HE IS ABLE TO
HELP THOSE WHO ARE BEING TEMPTED.

- HEBREWS 2:16-18

> **"I think there is a huge comfort knowing that we have a High Priest, as it says in Hebrews, that can empathize with our weaknesses. I love that because empathizing and sympathizing are two different things. When we say, 'I don't know how to do this. No one understands. Actually Jesus, as our High Priest walked this earth and went through everything we went through, never sinned, but experienced difficult things constantly. So he doesn't just say, 'Oh, I feel bad for you,' but says that he can actually empathize."**

JEREMY CAMP

I BELIEVE I DO

Oswald Chambers wrote: "If you obey God in the first thing he shows you, then he instantly opens up the next truth to you. ... Don't say, 'I suppose I will understand these things someday!' You can understand them now! It is not study that brings understanding to you, but obedience. Even the smallest bit of obedience opens Heaven, and the deepest truths of God immediately become yours."

An exercise that allows for a sobering reality for any Christian is to write on a piece of paper the heading of "I Believe." Next, as quickly as possible, jot down statements of personal belief. Some examples might be "Pray each day" and "Witness to my co-workers."

When finished writing as many beliefs as come to mind, next, write another heading of "I Do." Coordinating with each belief, then write down the reality of that belief—the action that coincides with the belief.

Based on Jesus's teaching and James's writing, what any of us would write down under the "I Do" column is what we *actually believe*. Thank God that his grace covers our shortcomings. But there are times that we need a timely wake-up call to challenge us to (or back to) "do what it says" and "put his words into practice." True change rarely comes without some pain.

Isn't it interesting that the centuries-old response to marriage vows at the altar is not "I Believe" but "I Do"? ∎

TRULY I TELL YOU,
WHATEVER YOU DID
FOR ONE OF THE LEAST
OF THESE, YOU DID
FOR *me*

getting personal

WHY DO YOU THINK ACTIONS ARE ALWAYS THE ULTIMATE TEST OF KNOWING THAT ANYONE MEANS WHAT THEY CONFESS OR BELIEVE?

WHY DO STRAIGHTFORWARD PASSAGES SUCH AS JAMES 1:22 AND MATTHEW 7:24-27 SOMETIMES BECOME DIFFICULT FOR US TO FACE THEIR TRUTHS?

BUT WITH THOSE SAME PASSAGES, HOW CAN TRUTHS LIKE THOSE HELP US CLEARLY KNOW WHAT GOD'S ULTIMATE GOAL IS FOR US AS HIS DISCIPLES?

WHAT ARE YOUR THOUGHTS ON THESE STATEMENTS? "…ONCE WE READ A TRUTH IN GOD'S WORD OR HEAR IT TAUGHT TO US, WE BECOME RESPONSIBLE FOR THAT WORD. WE BECOME STEWARDS OF GOD'S WORD IN OUR LIVES."

HOW DOES JEREMY'S QUOTE ABOUT JESUS CREATING EMPATHY FOR US BY HIS LIFE, RATHER THAN HAVING MERE SYMPATHY, ENCOURAGE YOU TO TRUST HIM MORE?

IN RESPONSE TO THE "I BELIEVE" AND "I DO" CONCEPT, WHAT IS ONE ACTION YOU HAVE TAKEN LATELY THAT LINES UP WITH YOUR BELIEFS?

WHAT IS ONE ACTION YOU KNOW YOU NEED TO TAKE TO LINE UP WITH YOUR BELIEF?

Day 33

REFLECTING REDEMPTION

Today is our final day in James chapter 1, building on the past four days.

(You might want to read verses 1 to 25 in your own Bible before beginning today for total context. Otherwise, start here.)

> ANYONE WHO LISTENS TO
> THE WORD BUT DOES NOT DO
> WHAT IT SAYS IS LIKE SOMEONE
> WHO LOOKS AT HIS FACE IN A
> MIRROR AND, AFTER LOOKING
> AT HIMSELF, GOES AWAY AND
> IMMEDIATELY FORGETS WHAT HE
> LOOKS LIKE. BUT WHOEVER LOOKS
> INTENTLY INTO THE PERFECT
> LAW THAT GIVES FREEDOM, AND
> CONTINUES IN IT—NOT
> FORGETTING WHAT THEY HAVE
> HEARD, BUT DOING IT—THEY WILL
> BE BLESSED IN WHAT THEY DO.
>
> - JAMES 1:23-25

When you see yourself in a mirror and then "go away," the image immediately disappears because the object of reflection is gone. That exact moment in time of what your hair looked like, the clothing you had on, the new wrinkle under your eye, or the zit on your chin will eventually fade from your memory.

The analogy is if you give God's Word only an occasional glance when you feel like it or if you have time, you won't remember what it says, and you certainly are not likely to live out its truths.

In verse 25, the phrase "looks intently into the perfect law that gives freedom" means to proactively seek out what you read or hear and decide how you can apply that truth. You consider what needs to change in you based solely on what it says.

To personalize this idea, you will be blessed in what you do if you look intently into the perfect law. Because:

1) You read, study, and seek God's truth.
2) You continue on in this regular discipline.
3) You don't forget what you've heard because the truth becomes yours.
4) You put that truth into practice in your life, bringing about blessing.

Here's a simple alliteration to help you remember the continual practice of the maturing believer:

• Seek God's truth
• Study God's truth
• Speak God's truth
• Show God's truth

Next, here's an analogy to help us understand how this works day-to-day.

DRIVING FORCE

Have you ever been driving on a long trip and gone into deep thought for many miles? You weren't distracted. You weren't looking away. You didn't doze off. You stayed in your lane at the right speed. Your eyes were focused straight down the highway. But suddenly, almost like you came back to reality, you realized you didn't remember the past few minutes.

At other times on the trip, you checked the mirrors, maintained your speed, and watched the drivers in other lanes, all while having a conversation or listening to music.

But while you were lost in a daydream, how were you driving safely? Focused on a conversation and your favorite song, how did you manage to drive with no issue?

In both instances, the answer is you are experienced enough at driving that the activity became secondary and subconscious when other things came to the forefront. "The driver" in you took over and does what "the driver" knows how to do in an apparent involuntary state. This has become second nature to you out of the consistent experience of highway driving. (This phenomenon does not apply to texting.)

Applying James 1:23-25 over time and experience, the process of looking into and obeying God at His Word can become like driving a car on the highway. You are living your life, but he is controlling the activity because Christ is "the driver" in your spiritual life. After a while, his Word begins to be such a predominant and active part of who you are, how you speak, how you make decisions, how you respond, how you live your everyday life that it starts driving your behavior.

A church member who the pastor knew was still very immature in his spiritual walk came up to him after a service. The man proudly stated, "Preacher, I'm leaving tomorrow on a trip to the Holy Land. I wanted you to know that everywhere we go, the tour guide will read the Bible passage to us that coincides with the holy site. It will be an incredible experience."

The pastor smiled and said, "I'm so glad you will have that opportunity. I know the trip will be amazing. But I want to challenge you that when you return to commit to reading the Word right here and then live it out *everywhere* you go."

"Sometimes you have to just be obedient to just say, 'You know what? I made a commitment to the Lord to take a vow to stay committed.' In my relationship, it's sometimes out of obedience and walking through it even when the road is rocky. You can endure those things because the freedom will come through the obedience and through the trials. I know it's easier said than done, but it doesn't matter even how we feel, that's just what it is. And sometimes you just have to be obedient. God honors obedience and through that obedience you'll have peace. "

JEREMY CAMP

getting personal

WHY DO YOU SUPPOSE GOD CHOSE TO USE WRITTEN WORD TO
COMMUNICATE HIS TRUTHS WHEN HE COULD HAVE USED ANY METHOD
HE WANTED?

HOW DOES THE EXPLANATION OF LOOKING INTO THE MIRROR
FROM JAMES 1:23-25 ENCOURAGE YOU TO TAKE GOD'S WORD MORE
SERIOUSLY?

WHY DO YOU THINK BIBLE READING AND STUDY CAN SO EASILY
BECOME NEGLECTED IN OUR LIVES?

WHEN YOU READ, UNDERSTAND, AND APPLY ANY PASSAGE OF THE
BIBLE, HOW HAVE YOU SEEN THAT IMPACT YOUR FAITH AND BELIEF?

IN THE "CHRIST AS THE DRIVER" ANALOGY, WHAT IS ONE PRACTICAL STEP YOU CAN TAKE TO ALLOW GOD'S WORD TO HAVE A MORE ACTIVE ROLE IN YOUR SPIRITUAL GROWTH?

REFLECT

IN CLOSING, IF YOU DON'T HAVE A CURRENT BIBLE STUDY METHOD OR RESOURCE, TRY THIS SIMPLE EXERCISE:

FIRST, READ A SHORT PASSAGE OF YOUR CHOOSING. NEXT, AS YOU "LOOK INTENTLY" AGAIN AT EACH WORD, ANSWER THESE QUESTIONS:

WHAT DO YOU THINK GOD COULD BE SAYING TO YOU THROUGH THIS PASSAGE RIGHT NOW?

HOW CAN YOU APPLY THIS STORY OR TRUTH TO YOUR LIFE TODAY?

AS YOU READ GOD'S WORD, TRY USING THIS SIMPLE METHOD FOR APPLICATION.

Day 34

CALL TO ACTION

Congratulations on arriving at this final two days of *I Still Believe!* You have worked hard and invested time and energy into your journey with Christ that will reap spiritual dividends in maturity for the rest of your life.

Before you walk through your final Call to Action to process the content for the week, we want to encourage you to take the momentum of the last five weeks and continue on in the habit of daily, regularly, spending time with God for the sole purpose of maturing in your relationship with him. If you continue this daily regimen, much like daily physical exercise benefits, you can literally accelerate your growth in knowledge, wisdom, fruit, gifts, ministry, and all God has for you.

• DECIDE TO COMMIT.

Life is going to happen, and schedules will be interrupted, but as a rule, decide this time each day is worth your investment. If you miss a day or two, don't feel guilty, just jump back in and go.

• PICK YOUR TIME AND CHOOSE YOUR PLACE.

Finding the optimum time in your day and the most private place will help guarantee you stay consistent and succeed in your goal.

• READ THE BIBLE

Whether you read a few verses or an entire chapter a day does not matter as long as you consistently take in the Word of God. There are great reading plans available and even Bibles that accommodate a

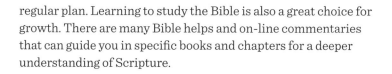

regular plan. Learning to study the Bible is also a great choice for growth. There are many Bible helps and on-line commentaries that can guide you in specific books and chapters for a deeper understanding of Scripture.

• PRAY

Like daily Bible reading, prayer—talking, as well as listening to your heavenly Father is a vital part of the Christian life. Mark 1:35 says, *"Very early in the morning, while it was still dark, Jesus got up, left the house and went off to a solitary place, where he prayed."* If Jesus, as the Son of God, made prayer a priority, so should we.

• OBEY

As you grow in your relationship with God and as he speaks to you, take action on what he says. Scripture tells us that obedience is better than sacrifice. A great prayer is found in 1 Samuel 3:9 "Speak, Lord, for your servant is listening." ∎

WHAT BIBLE VERSE OR PASSAGE DID YOU MOST CONNECT WITH THIS WEEK? NEXT, WRITE DOWN WHY YOU FEEL THAT MESSAGE CONNECTED AND THE IMPACT IT HAD ON YOU.

WHAT WAS ONE TRUTH OR PRINCIPLE YOU BELIEVE GOD SPOKE TO YOU THIS PAST WEEK?

HAS GOD IMPRESSED ANY NEW THING ON YOU THAT YOU BELIEVE HE WANTS YOU TO BEGIN?

HAS GOD IMPRESSED ANYTHING ON YOU THAT YOU BELIEVE HE WANTS YOU TO SURRENDER TO HIM?

**WAS THERE ANY RELATIONSHIP IN YOUR LIFE THAT
YOU SENSED GOD WANTS YOU TO TAKE ACTION?**

A CHRISTIAN FRIEND YOU NEED TO ENCOURAGE?

A NON-CHRISTIAN YOU NEED TO MINISTER TO?

WHAT IS ONE TRUTH YOU LEARNED ABOUT
DEALING WITH GRIEF AND LOSS?

WHAT ONE STEP OF OBEDIENCE DOES GOD WANT
YOU TO TAKE TO CARRY OUT HIS PLAN FOR YOU?

WRITE YOUR PRAYER HERE

father,

Day 35

PREP & PRAY

I f you are using this Journal in connection with a small group study ... This should be the day of your final small group meeting for the *I Still Believe* study. We want to give you the grace and space for two things:

1. If you need to catch up on any days that you may have missed, this time will allow you to be sure you engage fully with *all* the content. If you were pressed for time on any particular days, use this opportunity to go back and review.

2. We want to give you an opportunity to prepare for your group meeting so you can offer all you need to contribute.

Preparation for Your Small Group Meeting

LOOKING BACK OVER YOUR FIVE DAYS AND CALL TO ACTION, WRITE
DOWN YOUR ANSWERS TO THESE QUESTIONS. IF ANY OF THESE
DON'T APPLY TO YOUR WEEK, SKIP TO THE NEXT QUESTION:

DO YOU HAVE A QUESTION YOU WOULD WANT TO RAISE TO THE GROUP
LEADER FOR FURTHER CLARIFICATION OR DISCUSSION?

WAS THERE ANY CONTENT YOU STRUGGLED TO UNDERSTAND AND
WOULD LIKE TO HAVE CLARITY? (REMEMBER—GETTING YOUR QUESTION
ANSWERED COULD HELP SOMEONE ELSE.)

DID GOD SHOW YOU ANY TRUTH OR PRINCIPLE FROM THE STUDY THIS
WEEK THAT YOU FEEL YOU WOULD LIKE TO SHARE WITH THE GROUP?

CONSIDERING THE SPECIFIC SCRIPTURES FROM THIS WEEK, DID YOU HAVE A
QUESTION OR COMMENT YOU WOULD WANT TO SHARE WITH THE GROUP?

DID SOMETHING SIGNIFICANT HAPPEN IN YOUR WALK WITH GOD THIS WEEK THAT YOU WOULD LIKE TO SHARE OR REQUEST PRAYER FOR?

HOW WOULD YOU SUM UP YOUR ENGAGEMENT WITH THE *I STILL BELIEVE* STUDY THIS WEEK IN ONE OR TWO SENTENCES?

Pray for Your Small Group

Take a few minutes to pray for your group meeting. Pray for:

- Your leader
- Each member
- Any ongoing requests of your members
- God to open your mind and heart to receive what he has for you
- Wisdom in what you need to contribute to your group's dynamic

If you are using this Journal for your personal study only

Today allows you the opportunity to catch up on the content if needed. The questions below are designed to help you evaluate your experience this week, as well as indicate any area that you may need to seek out help or share with someone. Remember—don't be shy about going to a pastor, church leader, or trusted Christian friend if you realize you have a need.

LOOKING BACK OVER YOUR FIVE DAYS AND CALL TO ACTION,
WRITE DOWN YOUR ANSWERS TO THESE QUESTIONS. IF ANY OF THESE
DON'T APPLY TO YOUR WEEK, SKIP TO THE NEXT QUESTION:

DO YOU HAVE A BIBLICAL OR SPIRITUAL QUESTION
THAT YOU WOULD LIKE TO HAVE ANSWERED?

WAS THERE ANY CONTENT YOU STRUGGLED TO
UNDERSTAND AND WOULD LIKE TO HAVE CLARITY?

DID GOD SHOW YOU ANY TRUTH OR PRINCIPLE FROM THE STUDY THIS WEEK
THAT YOU FEEL YOU NEED TO SHARE WITH SOMEONE IN YOUR LIFE? WHO?

CONSIDERING THE SPECIFIC SCRIPTURES FROM THIS WEEK, DID YOU
HAVE A QUESTION YOU NEED ANSWERED OR SOMETHING YOU FEEL
YOU SHOULD SHARE WITH SOMEONE?

DID SOMETHING SIGNIFICANT HAPPEN IN YOUR WALK WITH GOD THIS
WEEK THAT YOU FEEL YOU NEED TO SHARE WITH SOMEONE AND/OR
ASK THAT PERSON TO PRAY WITH YOU?

HOW WOULD YOU SUM UP YOUR ENGAGEMENT WITH THE
I STILL BELIEVE STUDY THIS WEEK IN ONE OR TWO SENTENCES?

Prayer Time

Take a few minutes to pray for yourself and anyone that God brought to your heart
this week or today in your evaluation. Ask God to open your mind and heart to
receive what he has for you and also for wisdom in any actions you need to take.

I PRAY THAT OUT OF HIS GLORIOUS
RICHES HE MAY STRENGTHEN YOU WITH
POWER THROUGH HIS SPIRIT IN YOUR INNER
BEING, SO THAT CHRIST MAY DWELL IN YOUR
HEARTS THROUGH FAITH. AND I PRAY THAT
YOU, BEING ROOTED AND ESTABLISHED IN
LOVE, MAY HAVE POWER, TOGETHER WITH ALL
THE LORD'S HOLY PEOPLE, TO GRASP HOW WIDE
AND LONG AND HIGH AND DEEP IS THE LOVE
OF CHRIST, AND TO KNOW THIS LOVE THAT
SURPASSES KNOWLEDGE—THAT YOU MAY BE
FILLED TO THE MEASURE OF ALL THE FULLNESS
OF GOD. NOW TO HIM WHO IS ABLE TO DO
IMMEASURABLY MORE THAN ALL WE ASK OR
IMAGINE, ACCORDING TO HIS POWER THAT IS
AT WORK WITHIN US, TO HIM BE GLORY IN THE
CHURCH AND IN CHRIST JESUS THROUGHOUT
ALL GENERATIONS, FOREVER AND EVER! AMEN.

EPHESIANS 3:16-21

REFERENCES

Ben Witherington, "Handel's Messiah—the Story Behind the Classic," Beliefnet.com, accessed December 3, 2019, https://www.beliefnet.com/columnists/bibleandculture/2009/12/handels-messiah-the-story-behind-the-classic.html.

"Order of Knighthood Ceremony," lordsandladies.org, accessed December 9, 2019, http://www.lordsandladies.org/order-of-knighthood-ceremony.htm.

Aaron West, "20 Inspiring Quotes About Worship," Mediashout, March 13, 2017, accessed December 9, 2019, https://www.mediashout.com/inspiring-worship-quotes/.

James Collins, Tears in my Heart, "Do You Believe in Easter?" (Maitland, FL: Xulon Press, 2005), 13-16.

Chaplain 81, "A Hero's Homecoming", Free From the Fire, accessed December 19, 2019, https://freefromthefire.wordpress.com/2016/01/05/a-heros-homecoming/.

About Us, Joshua's Mission, accessed December 19, 2019, http://joshuasmission.us/about-us.

William Booth, "All of Me", Bible.org, accessed December 20, 2019, https://bible.org/illustration/all-me.

Albert Schweitzer, A Treasury of Albert Schweitzer, First Edition (Seattle, WA: Gramercy, 1994), 114.

Carol Sallee, "Jesus Freaks: A Bible Study for Those Who Refuse to Deny Jesus," The Voice of the Martyrs Canada, accessed December 13, 2019, https://www.vomcanada.com/download/freaks.pdf.

Bethany Hamilton, Soul Surfer: A True Story of Faith, Family, and Fighting to Get Back on the Board, (New York, NY: Simon & Schuster, 2006), 135.

Doug Moore, "School Janitor Comes Full Circle With College Graduation," St. Louis Post–Dispatch, May 14, 2012, accessed December 17, 2019, https://www.stltoday.com/news/local/metro/school-janitor-comes-full-circle-with-college-graduation/article_1daddcb5-94cf-583b-b68b-19fb36338f38.html.

Max Lucado, "What Was Meant for Evil, God Uses for Good," Faithgateway, June 19, 2019, accessed December 17, 2019, https://www.faithgateway.com/what-was-meant-for-evil-god-uses-for-good/#.XfkvJS3Mwk4.

Allie Torgan, "Former Cowboy Flying Free Health Care to Those in Need," CNN, April 6, 2012, accessed December 17, 2019, https://www.cnn.com/2012/04/05/health/cnnheroes-stan-brock/index.html.

Matthew Henry's Concise Commentary, Genesis 1:31, Biblehub, accessed December 18, 2019, https://biblehub.com/commentaries/genesis/1-31.htm.

Katie Davis, "Authors," AZ Quotes, accessed December 18, 2019, https://www.azquotes.com/quote/1316332.

ABOUT THE AUTHOR

Robert Noland

Robert Noland spent ten years as a touring musician, songwriter, and producer in Christian music. After leaving the road, he became the Director of Operations of an international ministry producing Christian resources, managing all aspects of the organization for twenty years. During that season, he and his family planted three churches with Robert being the lay-pastor of the third for nine years.

In 1991 he began writing Christian resources and has since authored over one hundred devotionals, study guides, journals, and books across children, youth, and adult audiences.

Robert and his family relocated in 2011 to launch his own ministry. In 2014, he became a full-time freelance author and writer represented by WTA Media.

In 2018, he worked with Christian artist Bart Millard of MercyMe to write *I Can Only Imagine: A 40-Day Devotional* published by City on a Hill. Robert has written multiple titles in association with many faith-based feature films, such as *I Still Believe.*

After forty years in ministry, Robert's calling has always been to present the Gospel through all forms of artistic media. He lives in Franklin, Tennessee with his wife of 35 years and has two adult sons, both musicians. Visit RobertNoland.com.